Highlights™

Jumbo
Book of
Amazing
Mazes

HIGHLIGHTS PRESS
Honesdale, Pennsylvania

Get Ready for Amazing Adventures!

The mazes in this book are more than meets the eye.
Here you'll find:

- traditional mazes
- string mazes
- riddle mazes
- number mazes
- quiz mazes
- scavenger hunt mazes and more!

Before you get started, make sure your pencil is sharpened and an eraser is handy, because these puzzles are sure to make you think! And if you get extra stuck, **you can find solutions on pages 228–255.**

Are you all set for the a-maze-ing fun that is about to begin?
See you at the FINISH!

Penguin Path

This penguin is hungry! Can you help him slip and slide down the right path so he can fish for food? Be careful not to crash into any other penguins.

START

FINISH

Ants Dance!

These three ants have each dug a different path down to the dance party. Can you help each ant find its way to the party?

START

START

START

FINISH

In Plane View

These paper airplanes have all come in for a landing, but where? Follow each flight path to see where each person's plane ended up. Enjoy the ride!

Swim Home

Help the clownfish swim to its anemone.

START

FINISH

Following the Arrows

Follow the arrows to find a path to camp.

START

FINISH

Art by Kelly Kennedy

Catfish Trail

This town is mad about catfish! Find the fastest way to FINISH. Then go back and see how many catfish statues you can find throughout the town.

START

STOP

FINISH

Cat's Mansion

Start at the arrow and find a path through the house, passing through each room only once. You do not need to exit. Simply stop in the last room you visit.

BONUS! How many cats can you find in the house?

START

Here U Go!

Uh-oh! It looks like it's starting to rain. Help this unicycling unicorn get to the umbrella shop so he can stay dry.

START

DRAGON'S BREATH RESTAURANT

NO SMOKING OR FIRE BREATHING!

ROYAL TEA

KINGPIN BOWLING

UNICORN HORN JEWELRY

OPEN

GLASS SLIPPERS FOR YOU

YETI SKI SUPPLIES

LANCE'S LOCKSMITHS

UMBRELLAS 'R US

FINISH

King Arthur's Expedition

King Arthur is seeking the sword Excalibur. Help him find the path that leads him to the sword. Along the way, pick up the letters to find the answer to the riddle.

START

A

S

A

W

O

N

R

I

E

E

14

What does King Arthur use in the dark?

_ _ _ _ _ _ _
_ _ _ _ _ _

Quality Koala Tree

Help Max solve the koala maze.

FINISH

START

The Puck Stops Here

Syd is trying to score the game-winning goal. Can you help her find the right path to the net? The symbols will tell you which way to move.

Move 1 space down	Move 1 space up	Move 1 space right	Move 1 space left

Path 1   Path 2   Path 3   Path 4   Path 5   Path 6

Float Your Boat

Ben and Maria are looking for the canoes.
Help them find their way to the other side
of the river so they can get paddling.

FINISH

Art by Howard McWilliam

Scarf Hunt

Matt, Katie, David, and Grace chose a windy day for sledding. Their scarves have blown away! Use the clues to figure out whose scarf is whose. Then find four paths in the snow that will lead each friend to the correct scarf.

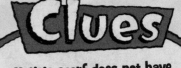

Clues

Katie's scarf does not have fringe. Matt's scarf has more than two colors. David's scarf is next to Matt's scarf. Grace's scarf matches her coat.

20

Nutty Squirrels

Follow the paths to see which treat belongs to each squirrel.

Piggy Problem

This little piggy got lost in a big barnyard. Help him find the path to his family so he can take a nice, cool mud bath.

START

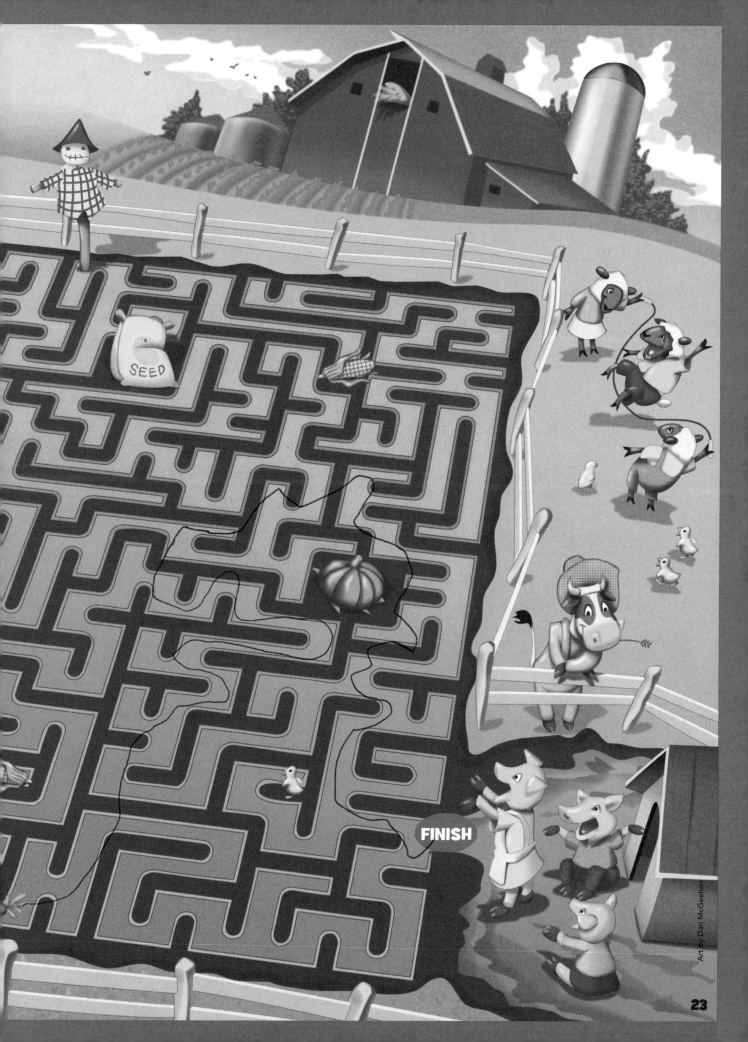

SEED

FINISH

Crab Walk

This hermit crab needs a new shell. Can you find him the path that will lead him to his new home?

START

FINISH

Tube Trail

Help this hungry hamster reach his treat!

START

GO BACK

FINISH

Kite Flight

Hold on tight! These kite flyers have gotten their strings tangled. Follow each person's string to see which kite he or she is flying.

Flower Power

Find a path from START to FINISH through the plants.

START

FINISH

Cat and Mouse Race

The cat and mouse are racing to see who can reach the kitchen first. The cat can only go through open doors and the mouse can only go through mouse holes. Time yourself to see who gets there first!

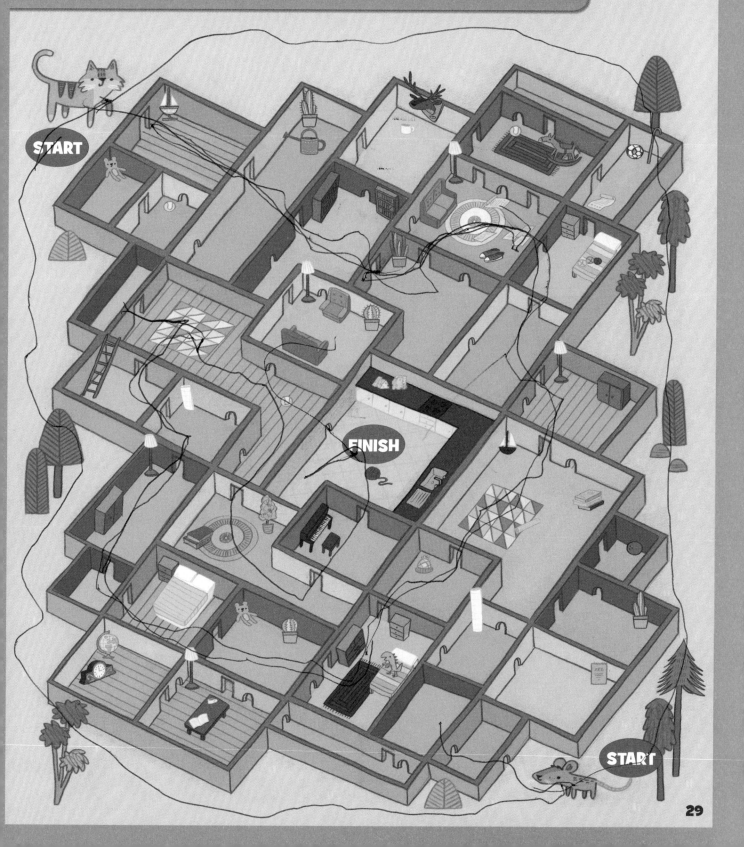

In Charge

Molly's electric car is about to run out of battery power! Can you help her get to the charger in time?

START

SLOW
CURVE
TURN

RECYCLE

FINISH

RECYCLE

Seed Scramble

Which plant grew from which seed?

Cop's Stop

Help this cop get back to the station.

START

POLICE

COURTHOUSE

HOTEL

POST OFFICE

LIBRARY

SCHOOL

POLICE

FINISH

33

Robot Party

Twigget is on his way to the annual Robo Ball. Can you help him find the way? When you've found the right path, write the letters along it in order in the spaces below to answer the riddle.

START

H
G
R
O
B
E
N
E
O
R
D
T
U
T
U
E
T

What's a robot's favorite party snack?

_ _ _ _ _   _ _ _ _

Art by Steve Skelton

Bus Stop

Ralphie is running late! Can you help him find the right path to catch the bus?

START

FINISH

SCHOOL BUS

BUS

Minus Maze

To find your way through this maze, subtract the first pair of numbers (**16−11**). Draw a line to the answer (**5**), then move to the next pair of numbers and do the same. The answers may be left, right, up, or down.

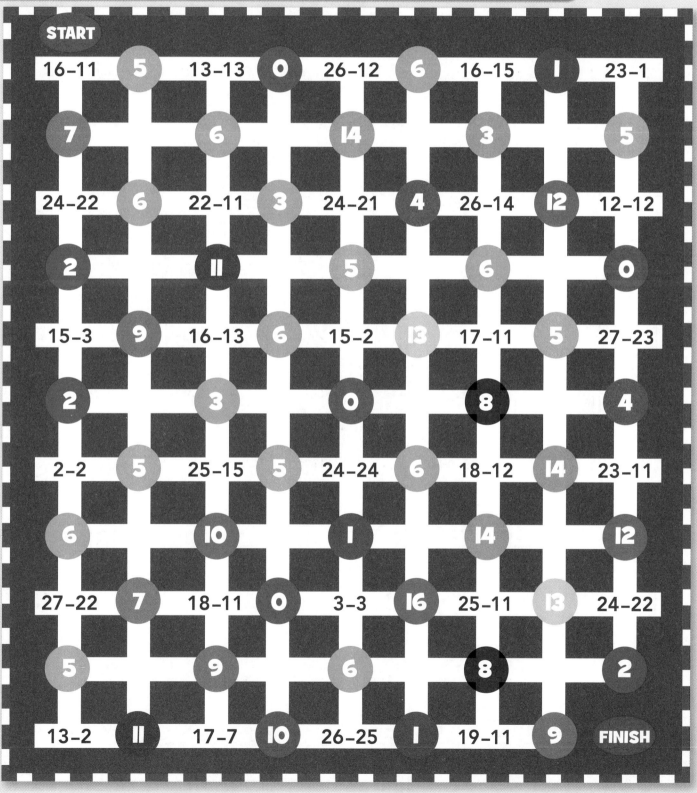

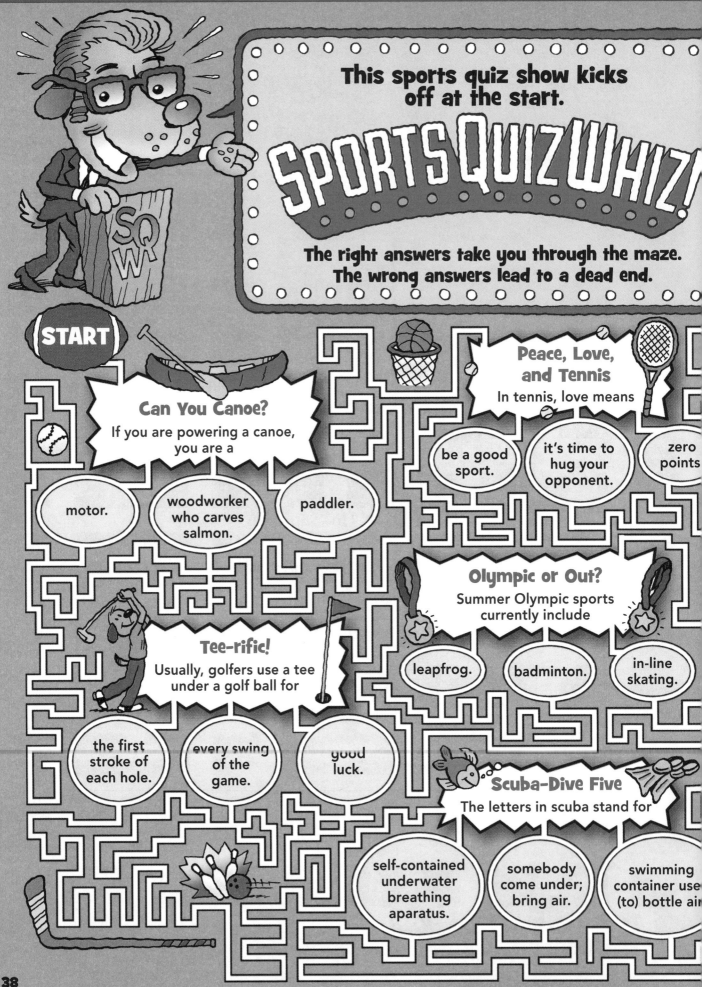

This sports quiz show kicks off at the start.

SPORTS QUIZ WHIZ!

The right answers take you through the maze.
The wrong answers lead to a dead end.

START

Can You Canoe?
If you are powering a canoe, you are a

- motor.
- woodworker who carves salmon.
- paddler.

Peace, Love, and Tennis
In tennis, love means

- be a good sport.
- it's time to hug your opponent.
- zero points

Tee-rific!
Usually, golfers use a tee under a golf ball for

- the first stroke of each hole.
- every swing of the game.
- good luck.

Olympic or Out?
Summer Olympic sports currently include

- leapfrog.
- badminton.
- in-line skating.

Scuba-Dive Five
The letters in scuba stand for

- self-contained underwater breathing aparatus.
- somebody come under; bring air.
- swimming container use (to) bottle air

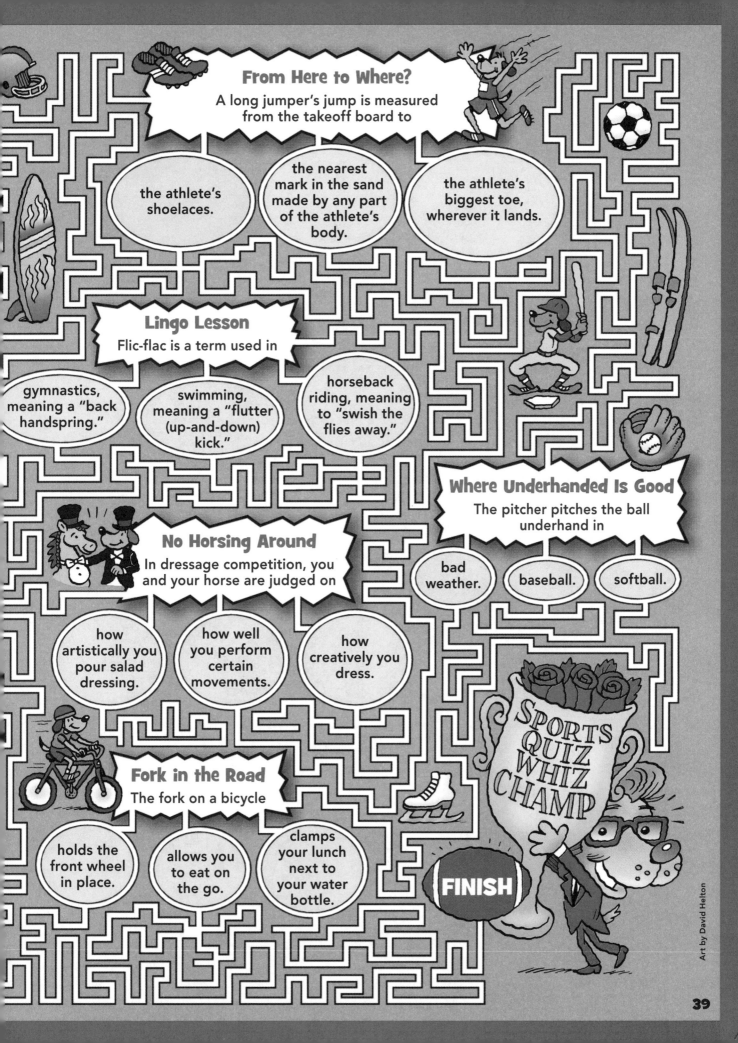

From Here to Where?

A long jumper's jump is measured from the takeoff board to

- the athlete's shoelaces.
- the nearest mark in the sand made by any part of the athlete's body.
- the athlete's biggest toe, wherever it lands.

Lingo Lesson

Flic-flac is a term used in

- gymnastics, meaning a "back handspring."
- swimming, meaning a "flutter (up-and-down) kick."
- horseback riding, meaning to "swish the flies away."

Where Underhanded Is Good

The pitcher pitches the ball underhand in

- bad weather.
- baseball.
- softball.

No Horsing Around

In dressage competition, you and your horse are judged on

- how artistically you pour salad dressing.
- how well you perform certain movements.
- how creatively you dress.

Fork in the Road

The fork on a bicycle

- holds the front wheel in place.
- allows you to eat on the go.
- clamps your lunch next to your water bottle.

FINISH

SPORTS QUIZ WHIZ CHAMP

Art by David Helton

39

Around Town

Welcome to Chillville. Find your way from START to FINISH, but watch out for one-way streets! On your way through town, see how many things you can find that rhyme with *chill*.

Plane Path

Follow the flight paths to find out which person is controlling each plane.

Which objects in the scene rhyme with *plane*?

Fun House!

Frieda and Freddy are in the house—the fun house! Can you help them find their way through it and back outside? Have fun!

START

FINISH

Mail Call

The postal dolphin has one last letter to deliver. Can you help him find the path to the mailbox? When you're done, write the letters along the route in the spaces below to answer the riddle.

START

FINISH

What is the best kind of letter to read on a hot day?

__ __ __ __ __ __ __

Extreme Bike Trails

The race is on! Find the quickest path to the FINISH line, but watch out for any obstacles.

Rodeo Roundup

It's Beginner Roping Day down at the ranch. Each newbie has roped something. But what? Follow the ropes to see what each wrangler has snared.

Navigation's a Go!

Voyager Dusk is blasting off to Planet Zatz. To get there, the ship must first pass through Planet Zoop and Zorka. Can you get it there while avoiding the black hole?

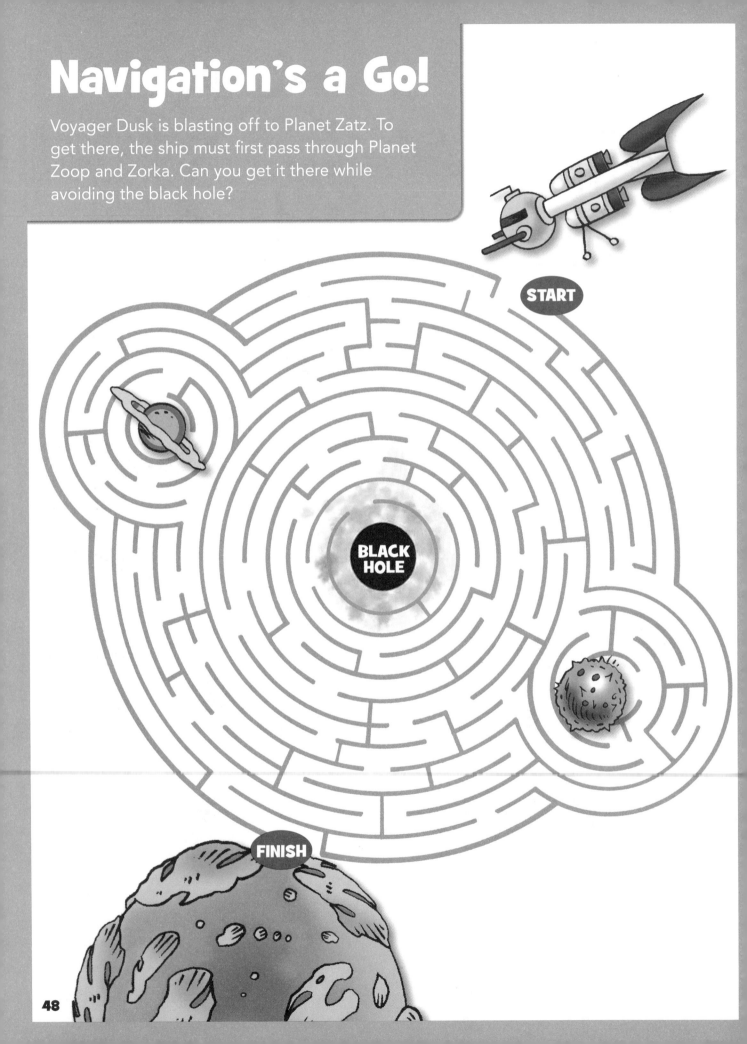

START

BLACK HOLE

FINISH

Water Ways

Help the swimmers get down the slide and into the pool, then see how many water-related words you can find on the slides at Wordy Water Park.

Grand Canyon

Maya and her dad need to catch up to their family. Can you help them find the right path?

START

FINISH

Let Down Your Hair

Rapunzel and friends, let down your hair! More princesses have come to save you! Follow each princess's hair to her rescuer.

Swimming to Atlantis

Andromeda is trying to get to Atlantis. Help her swim through the maze and to the FINISH.

FINISH

START

53

Sun Spot

This lizard wants to meet up with his friends at their favorite place to lounge in the sun. Can you find the path that will take him there?

Bonus Puzzle

Did you find the path? Now write all the letters you found on it in order in the spaces below. They'll answer the riddle.

What do reptiles wear on their feet?

___ ___ ___ ___ ___ ___ ___

Art by Jim Paillot

55

Meet the Beetles

All you need is love, and to find the quickest pathway to reunite Mingo with his friends.

START

FINISH

Party Path

Calvin has arrived at the location of his cousin's birthday party, but where is everyone? Help him get to the party by starting at the 9 in the top corner. You may move to a new box by adding 4 or subtracting 5. Move up, down, left, or right.

START

9	15	18	10	15	19
4	7	11	21	16	20
8	12	15	5	12	15
15	11	10	14	17	10
12	17	6	9	13	14
9	18	21	7	20	18

FINISH

Jungle Fun

Explorer Evie is hunting for the hidden treasure!
Three paths will take her there, but she needs to
pick up exactly 100 POINTS along the way. Use
the key to figure out which path will give
her enough points to take her safely to the
treasure chest.

KEY

Pile of coins
= 15 points

Key
= 20 points

BANANAS
= 10 points

Bottle
= 5 points

START

FINISH!

Garden Labyrinth

Find your way from START to FINISH through this hedgerow.

Start

1 What is the least number of arches under which you'd go to solve this maze?

2 How many things can you find that start with the letter "S"?

4 Are there more people on the correct path before the fountain or after it?

3 Can you spot five pairs of things that match exactly?

Finish

Where's My Sheep?

Little Bo Peep, Little Boy Blue, and other people in town thought it'd be fun to take their sheep to the market. The only problem is all the leashes got tangled. Can you figure out who each sheep belongs to?

Scavenger Hunt

Help Leo make it through the zoo's scavenger hunt. Along the way he has to take photos of three zoo animals. Can you help him reach each animal name and unscramble it? Once you've got each one, continue along the path until you reach the FINISH line.

START

OAKLA

LOGRA

GOONRAKA

FINISH

Art by Steve Skelton

Race, Car!

Can you help Racer Rex reach the FINISH line?

Splash Path

Grrrr-8! There's no wait for the waterslide. Find which watery path leads to FINISH. Then see how many 8s you can find in the scene.

Parking $8/day

AB8   123

Max. 8 People

Max. 2,800lbs

Min. 6 yrs. old

81

Buy 8 Tickets, get 1 free!

START

OPEN 7:30 am to 10:00 PM DAILY

SNACKS

Hot Dogs 98¢
8-Slice Pizza $4.00

Splash Zone!

Hard Turn 10 ft. Ahead

15

Splash Zone!

Ice Cream 8 Flavors

Splash Zone!

08

4:83.8

The Figure Eight

XII XI X IX VIII VII VI V IV III II I

Next Show 8:00

HATS - 2 for $8.00

T-SHIRTS - $4.98

FINISH

Disc Toss

Follow the path to see where each person's disc lands.

Leafy Maze

Brent and Lara have been raking leaves all morning, and now it's time for lunch. Can you help them find a clear path to their house?

START

FINISH

Rain or Shine

Talk about unpredictable weather! To go from this maze's rainy START to its sunny FINISH, you have to find the path that takes you through alternating clouds and sun. Your path cannot cross itself or go through two of the same symbols in a row.

START

FINISH

Gorilla Maze

Help Viola reach the gorillas.

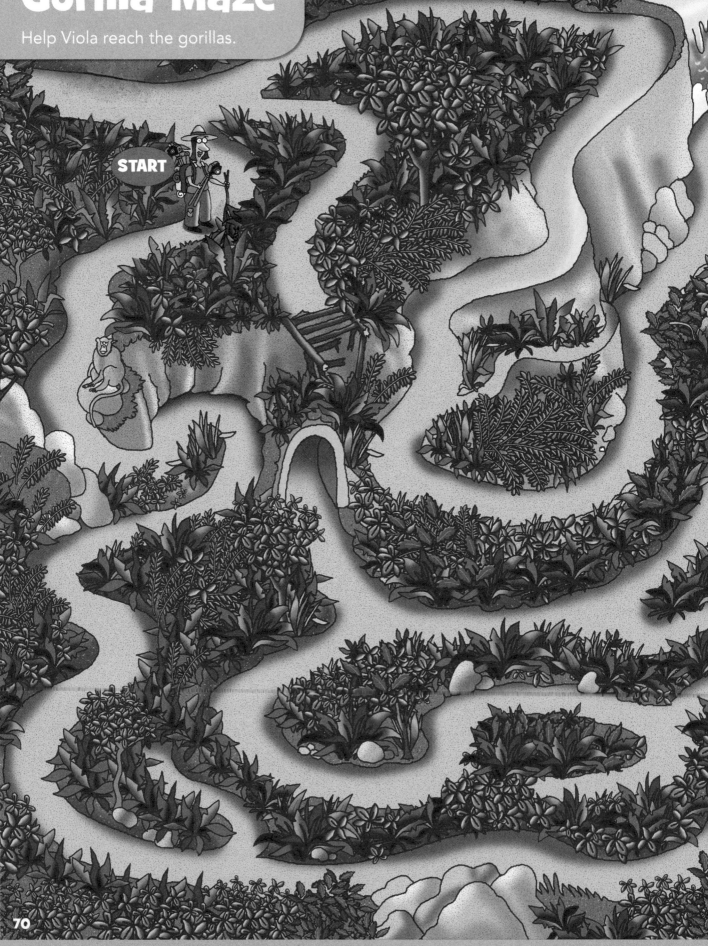

START

FINISH

Art by Steve Skelton

Reading Space

Do you know what astronauts like to read? Follow each line from a letter to a blank space and write the letter in that space. When you finish, you will have the answer.

M O K O C S B T O E

Ka-Yak Path

Follow the path so these yaks can get their kayaks in the lake!

START

FINISH

DOCKS

Ready, Set, Grow!

This community garden is growing in popularity. Can you help Rosemary meet her friend Tom so they can water their plants?

START

S T R A M D T N T P

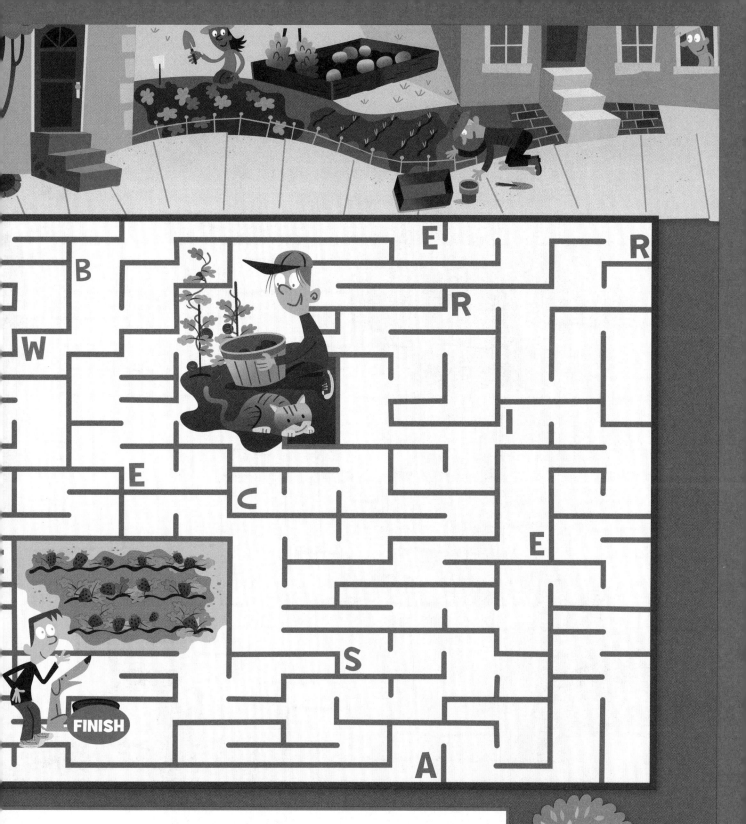

Bonus Puzzle

Once you've found the correct path, write the letters along it in order in the spaces below. They'll answer this riddle:

What is a scarecrow's favorite fruit?

___ ___ ___ ___ ___ – ___ ___ ___ ___ ___ ___

The Right Route

It's Groundhog Day, and Phil is late for his big appearance. Can you help him find the path to the top? Don't get grounded along the way!

FINISH

START

Pass Path!

Use the clues below to find a path from START to FINISH. How many paths can you find?

To play with a friend:
You each choose a ball along a border and put a penny on it as a marker. Taking turns, follow the clues and see who can reach the opposite side first.

CLUES:

Move 1 space in any direction

Move 1 space diagonally

Move 2 spaces left or right

Move 2 spaces up or down

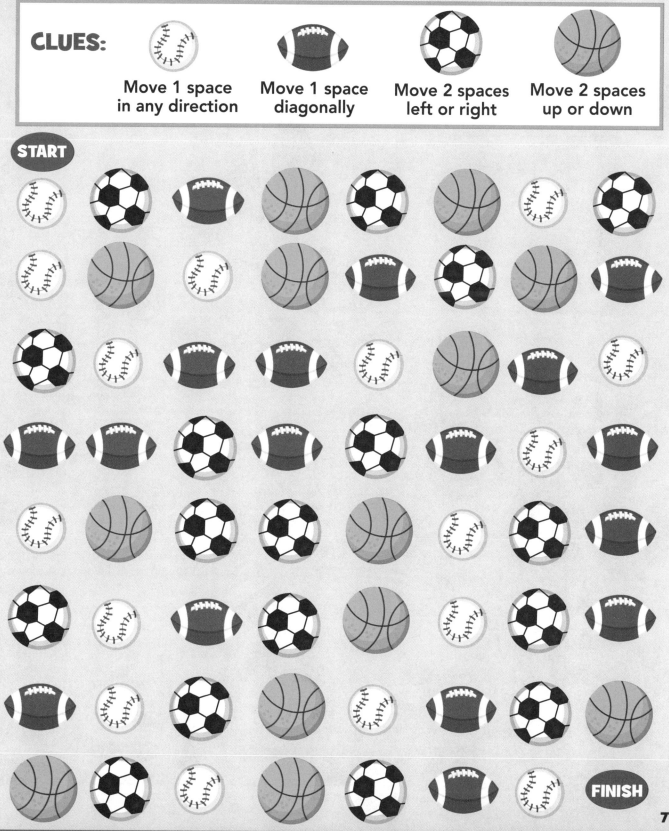

START

FINISH

Zippity Zoo

To be zoo volunteers, Suki and Lucas need to show what they know. Race with them from START to FINISH by answering each question correctly.

TRUTH OR MYTH:
An ostrich that's frightened buries its head in sand.

Myth   Truth

START

ALL IN THE FAMILY?
Like a poodle, pug, or pointer, a wolf is a

feline.   canine.

HELLO, "LITTLE ARMORED ONE"!
The armadillo is a

mammal.   reptile.

ZZZZZ . . . SNORT!
In 24 hours, a giraffe snoozes for

more than 15 hours, in long, deep sleeps.   less than 5 hours, in short naps.

BYE-BYE, BUGS!
How many insects can the little brown bat catch and eat in an hour?

60   600

MONKEY BUSINESS

To see a snow monkey in its natural habitat, swing on over to

Canada.

Japan.

THREE CHEERS FOR EARS!

One way to tell Asian and African elephants apart is that bigger ears belong to the

Asian elephant.

African elephant.

WHAT DO YOU CALL YOUR BABY?

A sea lion male is a bull, a female is a cow, and their offspring is a

pup.

calf.

A WHALE OF A WHALE

The blue whale, the largest living animal, can eat four tons a day of which food?

Dolphins and other mammals

Tiny crustaceans called krill

GARGLING REPTILES!

Which prefers salt water?

Alligator

Crocodile

FINISH

GREAT JOB!

Art by Mike Dammer

79

Coasting Through

Take this stomach dropping coaster all the way to the end!

START

FINISH

Knit Pick

Follow the yarn to see what everyone is knitting in the knitting group.

Sizzling Summer Maze

You just bought some ice-cream cones. Can you get to your umbrella on the beach before they melt? Begin at START and make your way to FINISH without backtracking or repeating any routes.

START

FINISH

Art by Robert Prince

Slippery Slope

Quacky is about to head down the slope.
Can you help him ski safely to the bottom?

START

FINISH

84

Construction Chaos

Find your way from START to FINISH on the busy construction site.

START

FINISH

The Rundown

It's time for the big All-State Cross-Country Race. Follow each runner to see what place she comes in. On your mark, get set, go!

Art by Daryll Collins

Puppy Pals

Follow each leash to see which puppy belongs to whom.

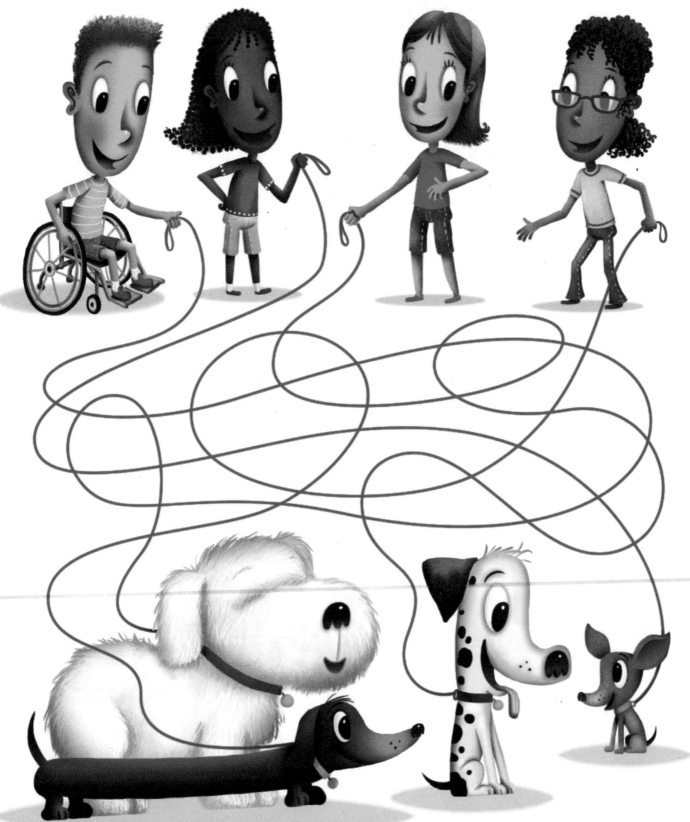

Uptown Dog

Fifi just moved into this fantastic 12-room doghouse. How can Fifi get from the front door to the back door by going through each room only once?

START

FINISH

Charm School

SNACKS

POPCORN

Fifi

Mall Maze

Robyn wants to buy a new pair of sneakers. Help her find her way from the entrance of the mall to the sneaker store.

START

GAME START!

BLUE JEANS

CARL'S CREAMERY

SALLY'S

Max's

GOLF EMPORIUM

THE COFFEE BEAN

SUNGLASS

SECURITY

PAUL'S PRETZELS

CANDY CASTLE

EXPENSIVE CLOTHES

JUST FORKS

NEVER ENOUGH TIME

HOT SAUCERY

FINE PERFUMES

MATT'S HATS

KAT'S KITES

Exit Strategy

You're at an amusement park with your family, and it's fun, except for all those totally terrifying rides. You don't want your little sibling or, ahem, anyone else getting scared. Can you find a way out of the park without scaring yourself—I mean, your little sibling?

ENTER

How to play:

Start at the ENTER and find the path to the SNACK SHACK without passing through any rides. Then exit the Snack Shack on the next page. Find the path to EXIT without passing through any of the four rides.

Art by David Coulson; background by Cobalt88

Got Space?

Renfru is trying to reach his home planet of Xylo by the time the three suns set on it. Can you help him find his way home? After you've found the way, write down the letters along the path in order in the space below to answer the riddle. Now get zooming!

START

C

S

A

A

P

A

T

W

D

Where will Renfru leave his spaceship when he reaches Xylo?

‾ ‾   ‾   ‾ ‾ ‾ ‾ ‾ ‾   ‾ ‾ ‾ ‾ ‾

Letter Drop

Only six of the letters in the top line will work their way through this maze to land in the numbered squares at the bottom. Write the letter in the lined space above the matching number to answer the riddle below.

| R | A | T | H | O | Z | P | R | C | S | K | O | E |

1 2 3 4 5 6

What animal always sleeps with its shoes on?

___ ___ ___ ___ ___ ___
1   2   3   4   5   6

Add It Up

To find your way through this maze, add the first pair of numbers (6+5). Draw a line to the answer (11), then move to the next pair of numbers and do the same. Answers may be to the left, right, up, or down.

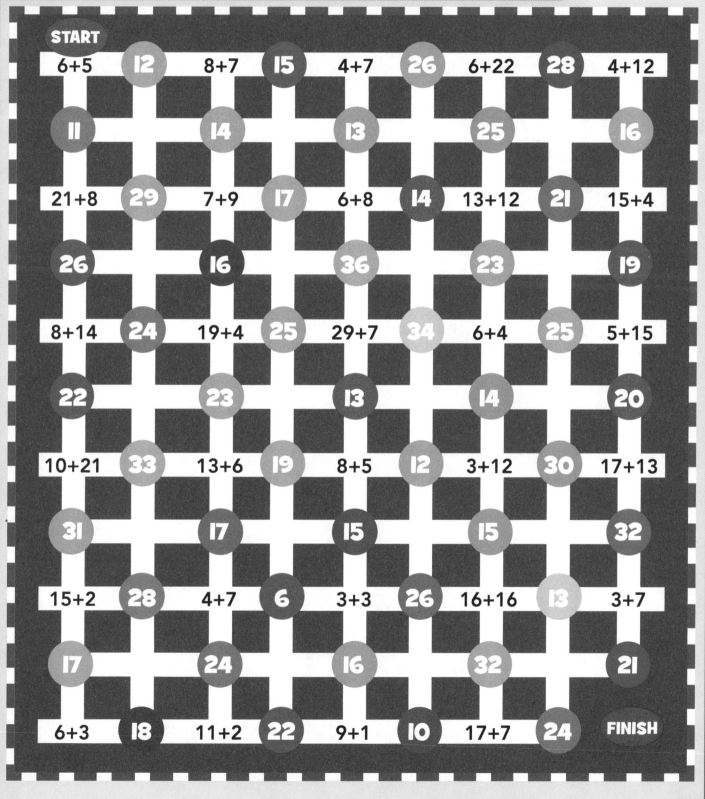

START

6+5	12	8+7	15	4+7	26	6+22	28	4+12
11		14		13		25		16
21+8	29	7+9	17	6+8	14	13+12	21	15+4
26		16		36		23		19
8+14	24	19+4	25	29+7	34	6+4	25	5+15
22		23		13		14		20
10+21	33	13+6	19	8+5	12	3+12	30	17+13
31		17		15		15		32
15+2	28	4+7	6	3+3	26	16+16	13	3+7
17		24		16		32		21
6+3	18	11+2	22	9+1	10	17+7	24	FINISH

Road Trip Trivia

Scooter and Skeeter need your help to win the "Road Trip Trivia" contest.
Show them the path from START to FINISH by answering each question correctly.

START

When you tour the capital of Washington, where are you?

Olympia   Seattle

You take a trip down the entire Mississippi River. Where d you first board your boat?

Minnesota

South Dakota

If you visit the coast of California, which ocean splashes you?

Atlantic   Pacific

From the southern border of Utah, which state can you see?

Arizona   Montana

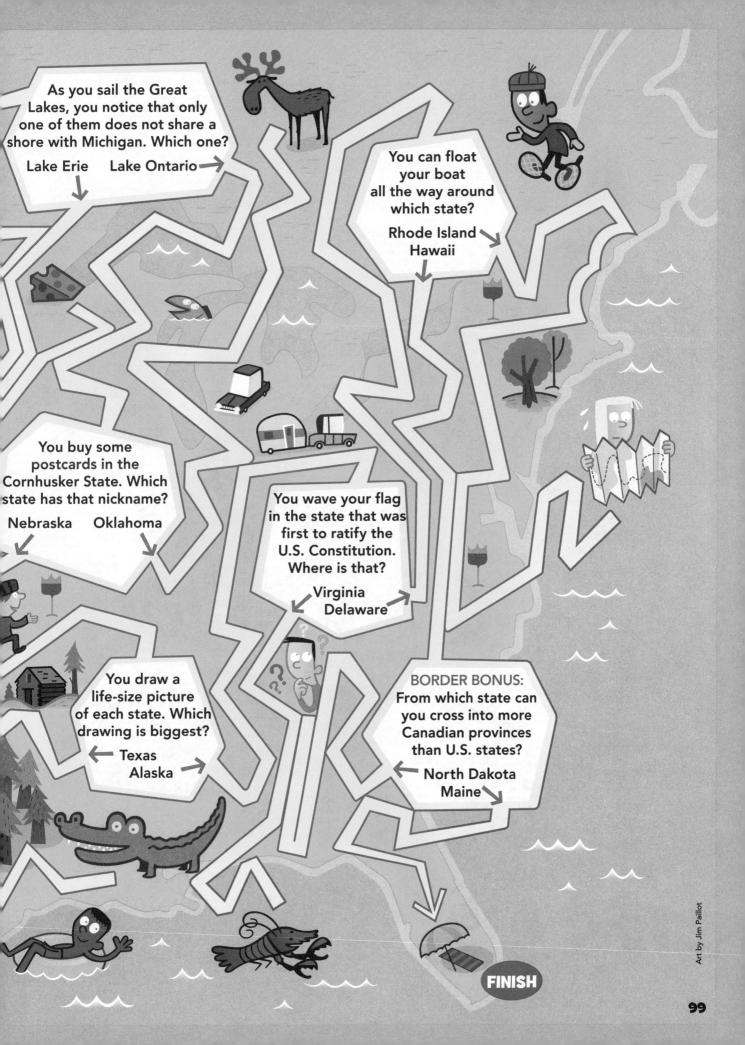

Cutting through the Crowd

Matt was just called onstage for the trivia contest! Help him find his way through the crowd. Then see if you can spot at least 20 things or people making different sounds.

START

FINISH

CONES

SNOWIES

POP CORN

Catch This!

Thwack! It's a high fly ball. Will it get over the fence? Follow the path of the ball to see if anyone can make the catch.

Swing Your Partner

This hoedown is in full swing, and Cowboy Mike's date is already in the middle of the dance floor. Help him find a path to her.

START

FINISH

103

Carrot Crunch

Help Carl Cottontail find the right path to get his prized carrot to the State Fair Carrot-Growing Contest.

STATE FAIR
CARROT-GROWING CONTEST

START

FINISH

Hedging a Path

Which hedgehog's chute leads to FINISH? Follow them to find out.
The hedgehogs can travel up, down, and sideways.

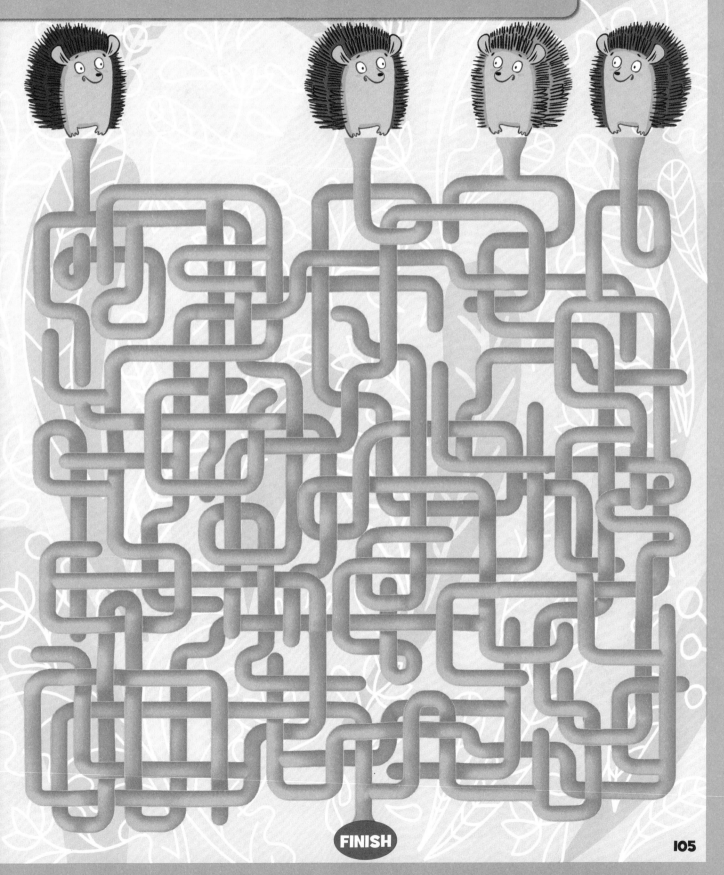

FINISH

Tangled Tunes

These critters danced their way into an earbud tangle! Follow each cord to see whose music is whose.

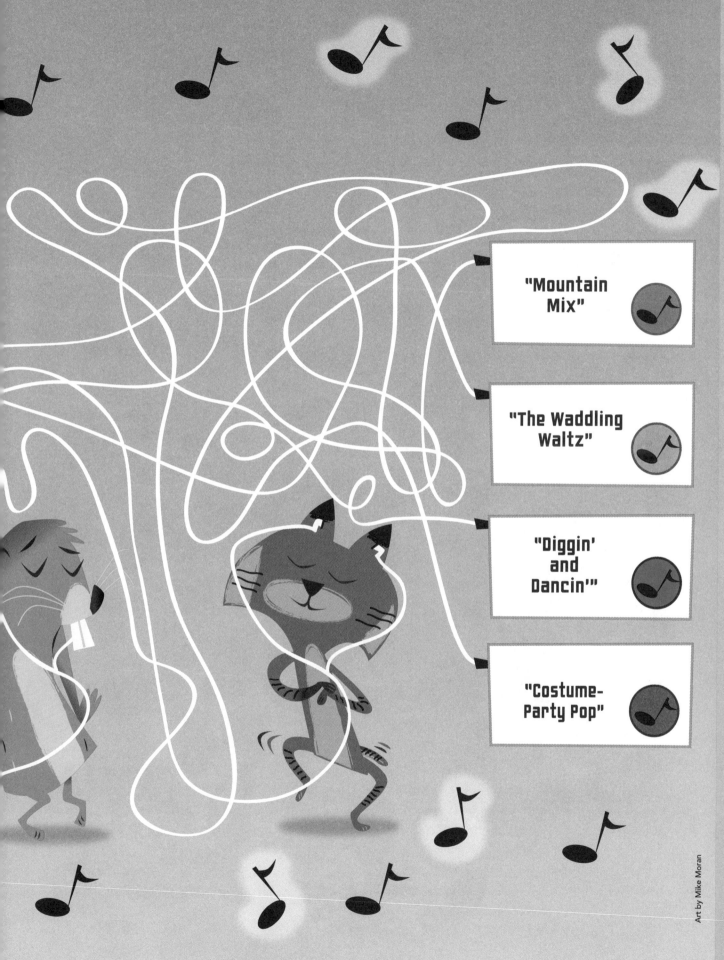

"Mountain Mix"

"The Waddling Waltz"

"Diggin' and Dancin'"

"Costume-Party Pop"

Germ Path

Find your way from START to FINISH. Then find all the matching pairs. Each of these imaginary germs has an exact match except one.

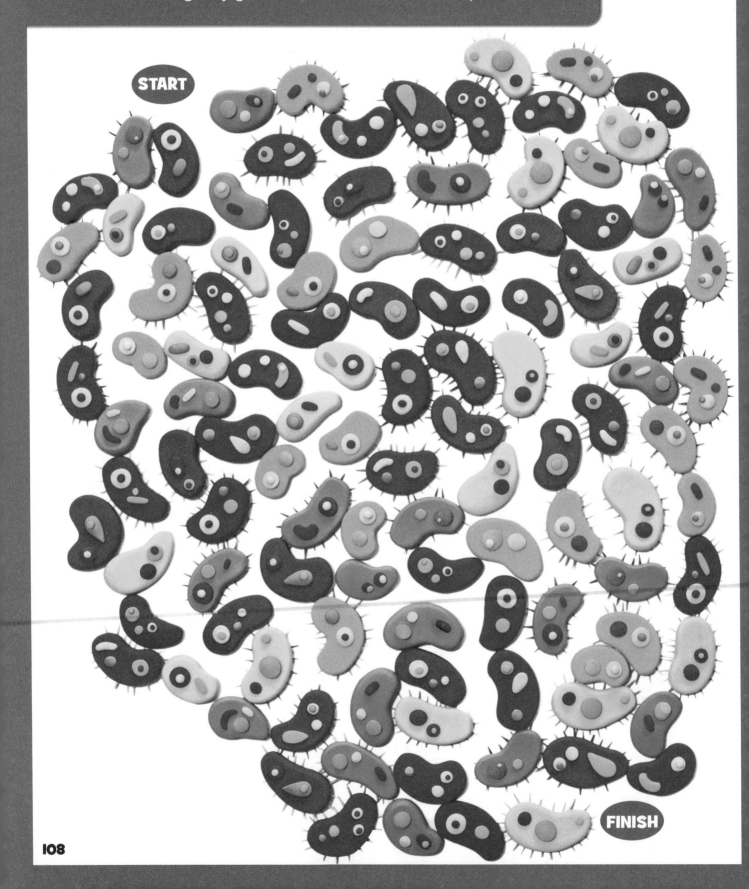

Construction Climb

Becky needs to get to the top of the construction site, but she can only go up the blue ladders and down the orange ladders. Can you find what path she will have to take to get to the top?

FINISH

START

Park Maze

Can you help Mike and Mia meet up with their friends? Find a clear path from START to FINISH.

START

FUN HOUSE

FINISH

Art by Steve Skelton

111

Rock It!

These rock climbers got their ropes tangled. Can you set them straight? Follow each rope from the climber on the mountain to find out who his or her partner is.

Haunted House

You may feel a little ghoulish that you got stuck up at the top of this haunted house. I mean you're turning ghostly from fear. But don't worry—you can *booook* it out the front door. Try to avoid as many ghosts and goblins as you can on the way out!

Golden Egg Hunt

Can you help Morgan and Max find their way to the golden egg? Collect the letters along the correct path to find out the answer to the riddle.

Why shouldn't you tell an egg a joke? Because it might

__ __ __ __ __ __ __!

FINISH

Two Points

Marissa and Matthew are meeting up at the rec center to shoot hoops.
Can you help each of them find a path to the court?

The Mane Route

Brady and his trusty horse, Heywood, are heading back to the stable. Can you help them find the right trail? The symbols will tell you which way to move.

Move 1 space down

Move 1 space up

Move 1 space right

Move 1 space left

Trail 1 Trail 2 Trail 3 Trail 4 Trail 5 Trail 6

Ocean Explorations

Find your way to the bottom of the ocean by answering each question. The right answers will take you through the maze. The wrong answers will lead you to a dead end.

START

1
Which is the largest ocean?

Pacific

Atlantic

3
What is the largest animal on our planet?

Great white shark

Blue whale

2
The Great Barrier Reef is off the coastline of

Chile.

Australia.

5 How many hearts does an octopus have?

2 hearts

3 hearts

6 The Pacific Ocean is circled by the "Ring of Fire." Why is it called the Ring of Fire?

Because the sun setting on the ocean looks like fire

Because there are active volcanoes around this ocean

7 How many plant and wildlife species in the ocean do scientists say we may have yet to discover?

9 million

9 billion

4 Which ocean is the warmest?

Indian

Pacific

8 What is the deepest place in the ocean called?

Deep Challenge

Challenger Deep

Art by Shaw Nielsen

FINISH

119

Ant Eater

Can you help this ant find its way to the food?
Try not to get too antsy along the way!

FINISH

START

Space Landing

Help these spaceships find their home planet!

An Uphill Climb

Which path will get the hikers to the top of the mountain?

START

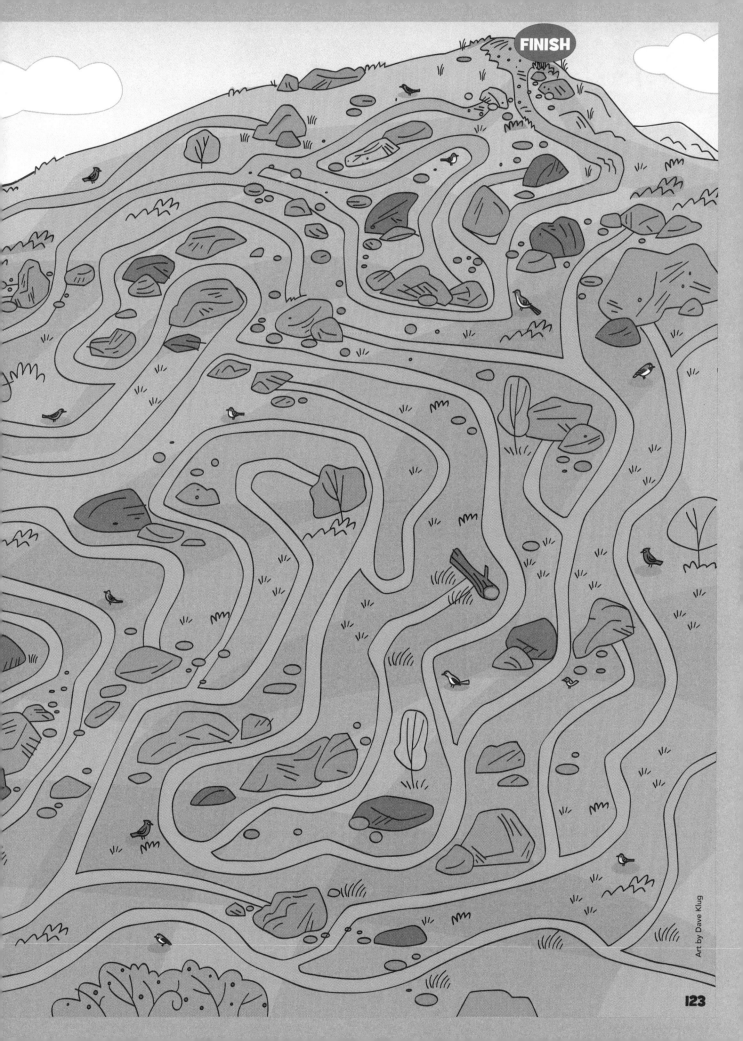

Art by Dave Klug

Castle Crawl

Isn't this one sandy, dandy castle? No one will be crabby if you help Clyde crawl his way from START to FINISH.

Wombat Path

Help Wally work his way through this maze and to the flowers on the other side.

START

FINISH

On Target

Robin Hood and his merry men are having an archery tournament. Can you trace the paths from arrow to archer to see which archer hit the target and wins the golden arrow?

Fireworks

Help the firefly find a path through these fireworks.

START

FINISH

Banana Phones

The monkeys all have their wires crossed. Help them untangle their phone lines before they go bananas.

Sheep-Shearing Season

It's sheep-shearing season. (Can you say that three times fast?) Dudley and his sheepdog, Zip, are herding their flock to the shearing shed. Can you help them find their way?

START

FINISH

131

Weight a Second!

Emma weighs 78 pounds. She has to take three 1-pound bowling pins across a bridge that will only hold 80 pounds. How can she do it? Follow each line from a letter to a blank space and write the letter in that space. When you are finished, you will have the answer.

Transportation Trails

Find your way from the car, train, and tram to the airport. Time yourself to see which way is the fastest!

START

START

START

FINISH

FINISH

FINISH

Bottled Up

Ella found a bottle washed up on the beach. It has a secret riddle message inside! To find the answer to the riddle, first find the right path from START to FINISH. Then write the letters you find along the way in order in the spaces below.

START

What's the best place to dance at the beach?

_ _ _ _ _ _ _ _ _ _ _ _

Bull's-eye!

This parachute is floating to Earth. Can you help it land safely on target?

START

FINISH

A-maze-ing Myths

Nessie, Sasquatch, and Yeti are heading home from the Mythical Creatures Convention. Can you help each of them find their way home?

Space Race

Soar from START to FINISH by zigzagging around the solar system. Answer each question as you go. The right answers will lead you farther across the galaxy. The wrong answer will lead you to a dead end.

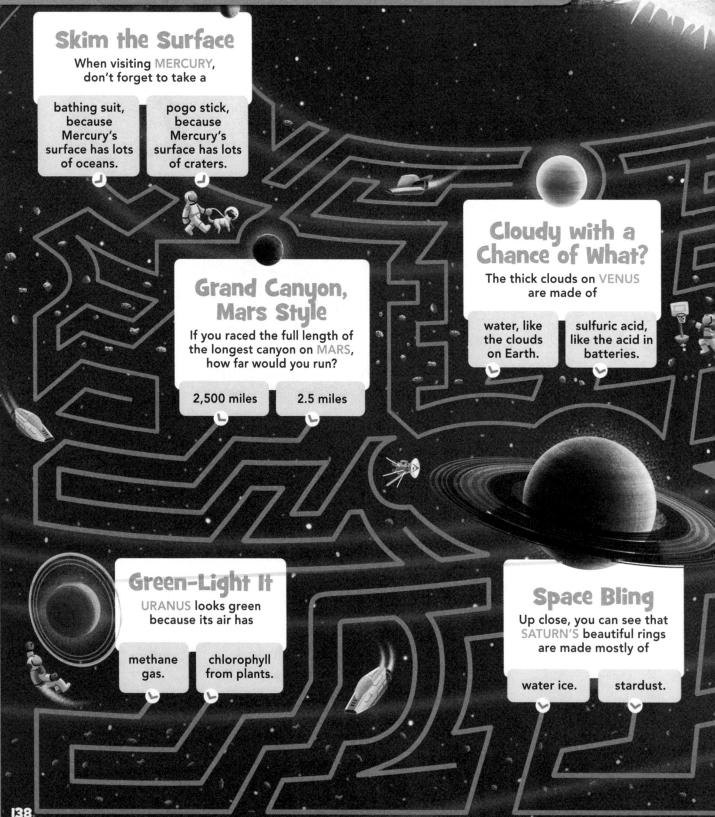

Skim the Surface

When visiting MERCURY, don't forget to take a

- bathing suit, because Mercury's surface has lots of oceans.
- pogo stick, because Mercury's surface has lots of craters.

Grand Canyon, Mars Style

If you raced the full length of the longest canyon on MARS, how far would you run?

- 2,500 miles
- 2.5 miles

Cloudy with a Chance of What?

The thick clouds on VENUS are made of

- water, like the clouds on Earth.
- sulfuric acid, like the acid in batteries.

Green-Light It

URANUS looks green because its air has

- methane gas.
- chlorophyll from plants.

Space Bling

Up close, you can see that SATURN'S beautiful rings are made mostly of

- water ice.
- stardust.

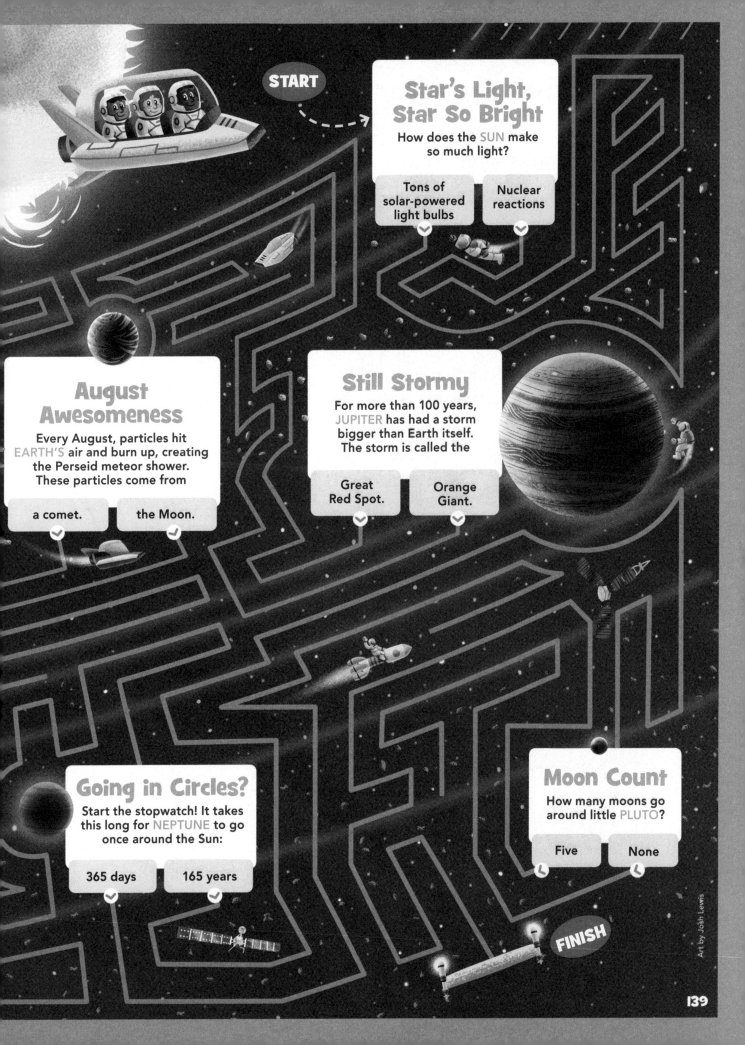

START

Star's Light, Star So Bright

How does the SUN make so much light?

Tons of solar-powered light bulbs

Nuclear reactions

August Awesomeness

Every August, particles hit EARTH'S air and burn up, creating the Perseid meteor shower. These particles come from

a comet.

the Moon.

Still Stormy

For more than 100 years, JUPITER has had a storm bigger than Earth itself. The storm is called the

Great Red Spot.

Orange Giant.

Going in Circles?

Start the stopwatch! It takes this long for NEPTUNE to go once around the Sun:

365 days

165 years

Moon Count

How many moons go around little PLUTO?

Five

None

FINISH

Art by Josh Lewis

139

EARS to You

Bite into this maze at START and nibble your way to FINISH without backtracking or repeating any routes. Stop at the five numbers in order along the way. When you're done, look at the maze to see a surprise.

START

FINISH

Cool Dogs

These prairie dogs are heading home. But who is going where?
Follow each tunnel to see which burrow belongs to which prairie dog.

Beware of Bears

It's salmon-spawning time in Alaska, and the bears are everywhere! Help this family get back to their lodge safely.

FINISH

143

Go Bananas

Have a bunch of fun working your
way through the banana maze!

START

FINISH

Traffic Jam

This bus is taking a trip to the museum. Get the bus around these crazy traffic jams.

START

FINISH

MERV'S

GRUNT'S GYM

UNLIMITED PANTS

MUSTARD SHOPPE

WORLD CORP.

THE PENCIL FACTORY

JAM

CARL'S COOKIES

Shelled Out!

These six eggs have just hatched. Follow the path from each shell to find out who—or what—hatched from each egg.

Wall Art

Make your way from START to END around each of the paintings.

Pet Snail Trail

Xu's favorite little pet store is a little unusual. The two elevators stop only on certain floors, and the slugs keep escaping from their habitat! Find the 15 caterpillars. Then figure out how many times Xu had to change elevators to complete his to-do list in order.

Xu's To-Do's

1. Buy pet snail.
2. Have snail groomed.
3. Go to gastropod obedience class.
4. Buy *Snail Without Fail* book.
5. Grab a seaweed-mushroom smoothie.
6. Take a photo with new friend!

As Far As You Can Sea

Dive into this maze at START and swim to FINISH without backtracking or repeating your route. Stop at the numbers 1 to 4 along the way.

3.

4.

FINISH

Art by Joe Wos

151

Astro Adventure

Find your way through the Imagination Constellations from START to FINISH. Be sure to avoid the satellites along the way. Then solve the word puzzles.

START

Riddle 1:
What do you call an almond on a spaceship?

Are there more blue (hotter) stars or red (cooler) stars?

Riddle 3:
Why did the Moon stop eating?

Riddle 2:
How do you get a baby astronaut to fall asleep?

Riddle 4:
What do astronauts eat for breakfast?

Unscramble this word to find out what kind of puzzle solver you are.

L A R S T E L!

FINISH

Oodles of Noodles

Help Henry bike through Spaghettiville to get to his friends jumping rope in Noodle Park.

START

FINISH

153

Scuba Time

You can make a big splash in this maze by finding the one path from START to FINISH. Once you've got it, write the letters you find along the route in order in the spaces below to answer the riddle.

START

Y

S

H

E

A

M

Y

B

A

O

G

O

U

Y

F

U

W

F

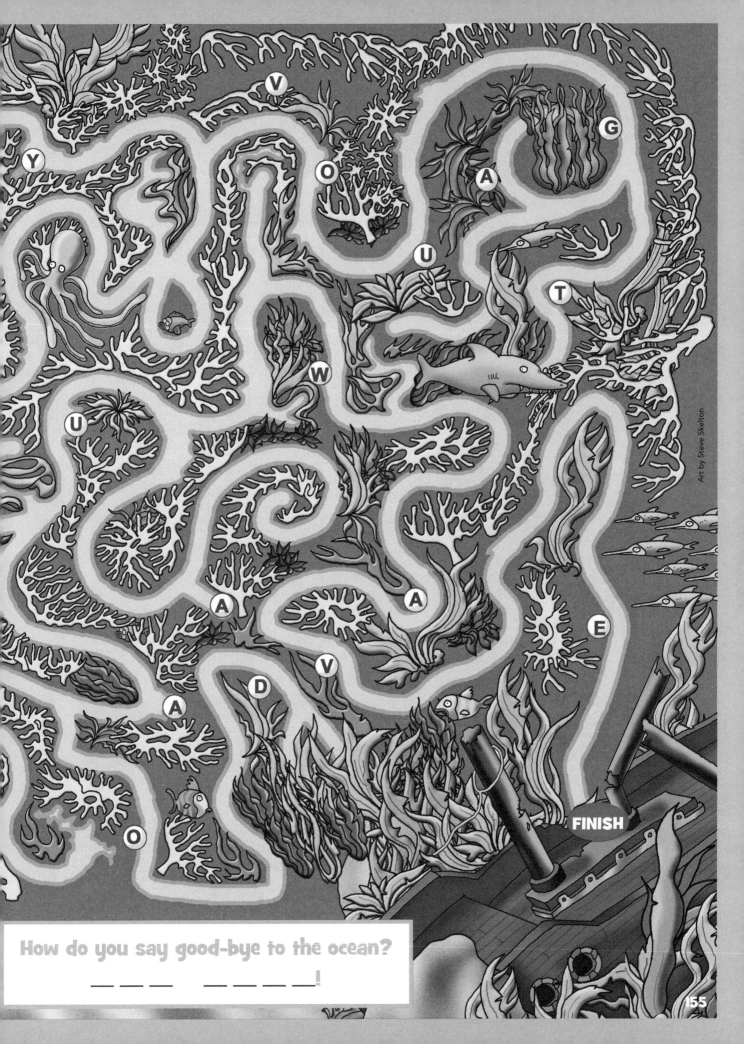

How do you say good-bye to the ocean?

_ _ _   _ _ _ _!

Letter Drop

Only six of the letters in the top line will work their way through this maze to land in the numbered squares at the bottom. Write the letter in the lined space above the matching number to answer the riddle below.

R A T Z E R O B C R K O A

1 2 3 4 5 6

If the alphabet goes from A to Z, what goes from Z to A?

‾ ‾ ‾ ‾ ‾ ‾
1 2 3 4 5 6

The Number-Nimble Bees

To leave the hive, the bees play a game: step only on two-digit numbers in which the digits add up to less than 10. Can you find the path that leads the bees out of the hive?

65 33 67 88 9 13 3 16 6 9 1 72 2 16
91 12 42 65 2 39 23 7 45 26 3 77 80
7 1 2 51 1 5 11 87 90 1 38 41 3 5
2 23 34 9 6 3 38 44 17 7 44 7 1
88 32 7 90 80 1 2 7 17 81 37 2 15 7
1 22 97 59 65 13 9 5 66 3 32 17 65
3 33 56 6 77 9 12 1 10 13 17 61 23 9
2 25 77 93 6 7 START 65 3 2 11 6 2
43 65 35 11 13 8 41 2 71 36 90 15 1 4
37 1 4 77 17 19 11 39 8 13 32 57 2
55 7 22 89 91 33 18 66 57 22 11 44 94 77
12 56 44 99 74 39 7 42 19 21 88 11 3
11 97 77 11 2 3 88 9 32 6 34 9 87 5
77 1 66 29 1 5 39 84 73 99 5 91 10
22 4 88 21 3 17 68 41 15 5 74 34 7 54

A-maze-ing Tractor

Help Tripp and Scout find their way through the tractor maze.

FINISH

Log Jamming

Grab your wetsuit! This log is about to take a plunge. Can you steer it smoothly all the way to FINISH without getting soaked?

START

FINISH

Balloon Bunch

These friends' balloons have gotten all tangled up. Follow each string to see which balloon belongs to which friend, then write the letter on the balloon on their T-shirts to answer the riddle.

What is a balloon's least favorite music?

Lost Luggage

Sandy has lost her luggage at the airport! Help her find it in the lost luggage room.

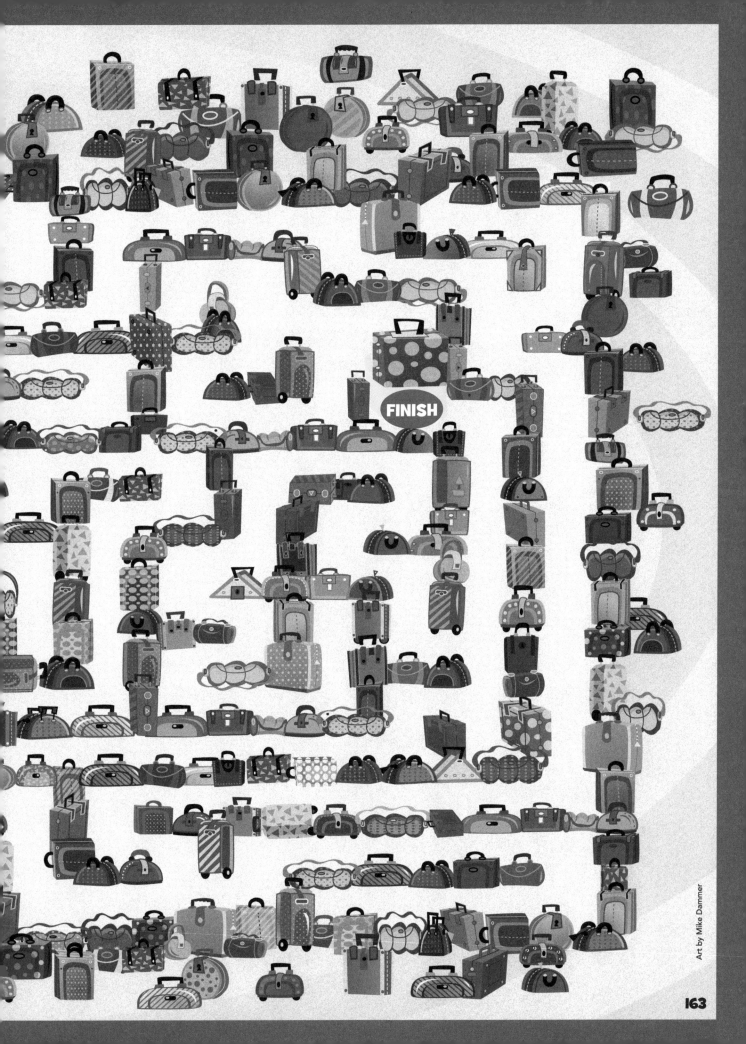

FINISH

Quilt Path

Make your way through the quilt from START to FINISH.

START

FINISH

Hamster House

Freckles is hungry. Can you help him find his route to the table?
(He can pass by papers and seeds.)

Bonus! Find 15 hidden seeds.

Super Bonus! How many words
can you spot that are spelled
with the letters from the word
HAMSTER?

165

Jump on It!

These jump ropers need to find their partner. Follow each rope to see who is partnered with whom. Go ahead, jump on in!

Bonanza Bakery

Barry's kitchen is full of orders, and there's still more to make! Can you help him find his way around all the baked goods and to the oven?

START

FINISH

Maize Maze

Find the quickest path through the corn maze from ENTER to EXIT. Then find a path that goes through every flagged checkpoint. Can you also find a path that goes through only even-numbered checkpoints?

Bonus!

Tom completed the maze and collected a letter sticker at each checkpoint. Can you help him unscramble the letters to answer the riddle?

Name: Tom

COLONEL SHUCK'S
CORN MAZE WORD SCRAMBLE

F D C I N O C L E R

What has thousands of ears but can't hear?

A _ _ _ _ _ _ _ _ _

Zebra Crossing

No two zebras have the same set of stripes. Can you get through these zebras' unique stripes from START to FINISH? Go through the numbers in order from 1 to 5 without back tracking or repeating any routes.

FINISH

Hook, Line, and Tangled

These lines got tangled! Can you figure out what each fisher caught?

Parrot Path

Weave your way from START to FINISH.

START

FINISH

Touchdown!

Wide receiver Justin Tyme fielded the punt. Now he's heading for the Bears' end zone. Help him find the one path that will bypass the Rams' defense and get Justin to the FINISH. Then write the letters you found along the path in order to answer the riddle.

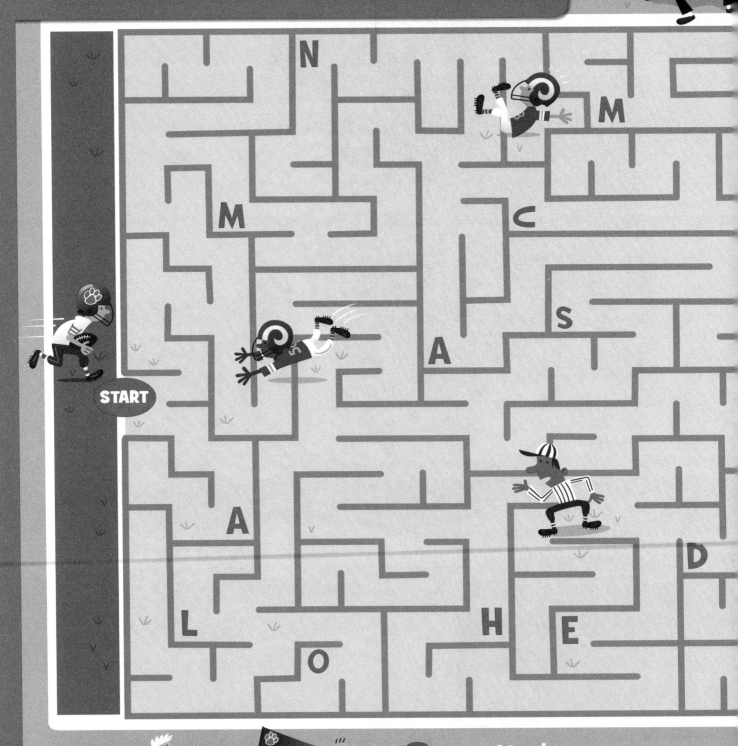

START

Tackle This:
Scout out 13 football helmets.

What did the farmer get when he let the football team practice on his field?

_ _ _ _ _ _ _   _ _ _ _ _ _ _ _

Art by Jim Paillot

Bus Stop

The bus has one last stop before getting to school. Can you pick up the kids waiting at the bus stop and then find the way to school?

START

BUS STOP

FINISH

SCHOOL

Magic Maze

Tricky Trixie has gotten lost on her way to her big magic show. Can you help her find the right path to the stage before her audience disappears? The symbols will tell you which way to move.

Move
1 space
down

Move
1 space
up

Move
1 space
right

Move
1 space
left

Path 1 Path 2 Path 3 Path 4 Path 5 Path 6

The A-maze-ing Time-Travel Trip!

Choose the correct answer for each question to travel through time. (The wrong answer won't get you far.)

START

Put It on the Map

President George Washington chose the site where this would be built.

White House

Statue of Liberty

The Write Stuff

Author Samuel L. Clemens was better known by his pen name,

Dr. Seuss.

Mark Twain.

What's Your Plan

Architect Maya Lin designed the Vietnam Veterans Memorial and the

Eiffel Tower.

Civil Rights Memorial.

Inventive Mr. President

Abraham Lincoln was the only president to hold a U.S. patent. The patent was for a device to

split rails into toothpicks.

lift riverboats over sandbars.

Planting New Ideas

George Washington Carver is known for finding new uses for crops like peanuts. Also a teacher, he designed

edible school supplies.

a movable wagon classroom to take to farmers and sharecroppers.

Civil War Work

Harriet Tubman led slaves to freedom on the Underground Railroad. During the Civil War, she worked for the Union Army as

a cook and nurse.

a photographer.

Touching Down!

In 1969, Commander Neil Armstrong became the first person to walk on the Moon. The lunar module he landed there was called

the Eagle.

Moon Walker.

Without Sight or Sound

Helen Keller, blind and deaf from early childhood, became a writer and a voice for others. She was taught by

Martha Washington.

Anne Sullivan.

You Take the Prize!

Albert Einstein, one of the most influential scientists of the last century, won a

Grammy Award for his chart topper, "Rockin' in Time and Space."

Nobel Prize in Physics.

Coin Trip

This female member of the Lewis and Clark Expedition has been pictured on a dollar coin since 2000.

Sacagawea

Laura Ingalls

FINISH

Art by David Helton

179

Ramped Up!

These pups are amped up from jumping off these ramps.
Trace each skateboarder back to the ramp he jumped from.

Recycle It!

Arun is headed to the recycling center. On the way, he has to pick up three bags of things to recycle. Can you help him reach each item and unscramble its name? Once you've got each one continue to FINISH where you can recycle everything you picked up!

START

SNAPPEREW

182

Dino Discovery

Follow the maze from START to FINISH through the dinosaur.

START

FINISH

Parking Lot

The parking lot outside the grocery store is packed! Can you help Tricia find her car?

Zoo Crew

Follow each path from START to FINISH to see where each group is going at the zoo.

Madagascar!

Tiger MOUNTAIN

CONGO
Gorilla Forest

Butterfly Garden

Art by Dave Klug

Checking Out

Mark has a huge stack of books to check out at the library, but he can't see over his pile. Can you help him find his way to the check-out desk?

EXIT

FINISH

START

Road Trip on Planet Paint

On Planet Paint, color rules! To travel around, you must leave any purple house by a road that's a different color from the one you came in on. How many moves will it take you to get from START to FINISH?

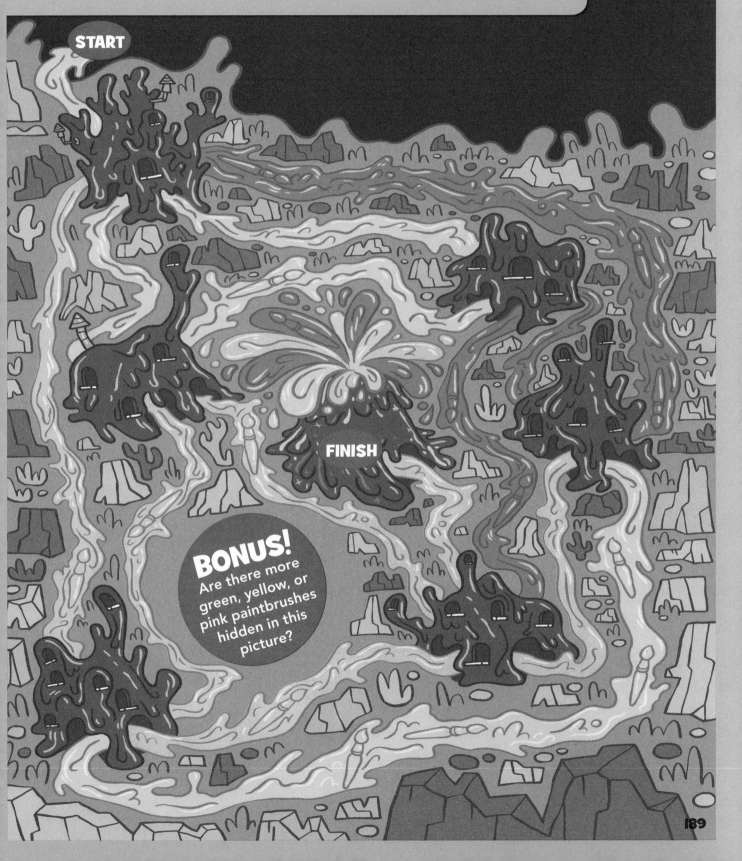

START

FINISH

BONUS!
Are there more green, yellow, or pink paintbrushes hidden in this picture?

Spelunking Splendor

People who visit this cave add their signatures on the wall. Help these spelunkers get to the wall so they can add their signatures, too. Then see if you can find space to add your own signature to the wall.

START

Campsite Sighting

Harriet took a walk in the moonlight, and now she needs help getting back to camp. Can you help her find the right yellow path? Careful—this maze may get a little in-tents!

START

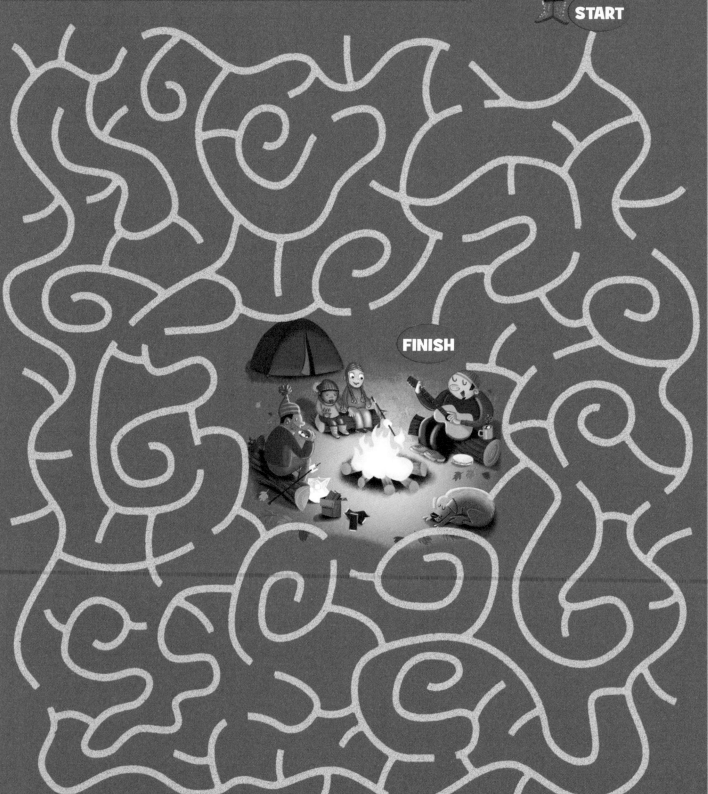

FINISH

Planet Parking

Help Astronaut Ally find her way back to her spaceship. Once you've found the right path, write the letters along it in order in the spaces below to answer the riddle.

START

FINISH

How do you have a good outer space party?

_ _ _ _ _ - _ _

Get Down

Jack is about to tackle the toughest trail on the slopes. Can you help him find his way safely to the bottom of the mountain? When you're done, write the letters you've found along the route in order in the spaces below to answer the riddle.

START

Why don't mountains get cold in the winter?

__ __ __ __ __   __ __ __ __   __ __ __ __   __ __ __ __ .

Movie Maze

Steven is meeting his friends for a movie. But first he has to find the movie theater. Can you help him find the path that will take him there? Hurry, it's almost showtime!

Time Trails

To find your way through this maze, multiply the first pair of numbers **(5x5)**. Draw a line to the answer **(25)**, then move to the next pair of numbers and do the same. Answers may be to the left, right, up, or down.

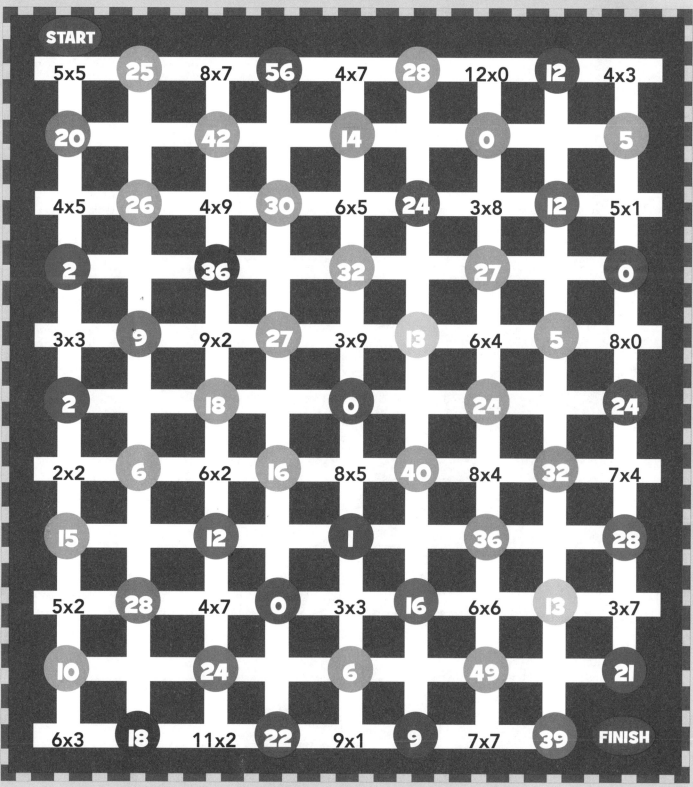

A-maze-ing Corn

Make your way from START to FINISH through the corn maze. Once you've found the right path, write the letters along it in order in the spaces below to answer the riddle.

What did the corn maze say when the scarecrow gave it a compliment?

_ _ - _ _ _ _ _ _ ,

_ _ _ _ _ _ .

Spider Web

Spencer the spider got home from a long day at the silk factory. Help him find his way through the spider web maze to get to his bed.

START

FINISH

Amped Up!

These musicians want to record their latest song. Can you help them figure out which instrument is connected to each amp?

City Traffic

Help the Robinson family find their way to the museum from the hotel.

MOVIE

DINOSAURS DINOSAURS

FINISH

Art by David Coulson

Letter Drop

Only five of the letters in the top line will work their way through this maze to land in the numbered squares at the bottom. Write the letter in the lined space above the matching number to answer the riddle below.

S O L W B I E R S H H I D

1 2 3 4 5

What is a basketball player's favorite cheese?

___ ___ ___ ___ ___
1   2   3   4   5

Castle Crisscross

Help Eli find his way across the castle from START to FINISH.

Pooch Puzzler

It's a furry flurry at the dog park. These dog owners got their leashes terribly tangled. Can you help each person find his or her dog?

Pretzel Path

Find your way around the pretzels from START to FINISH.

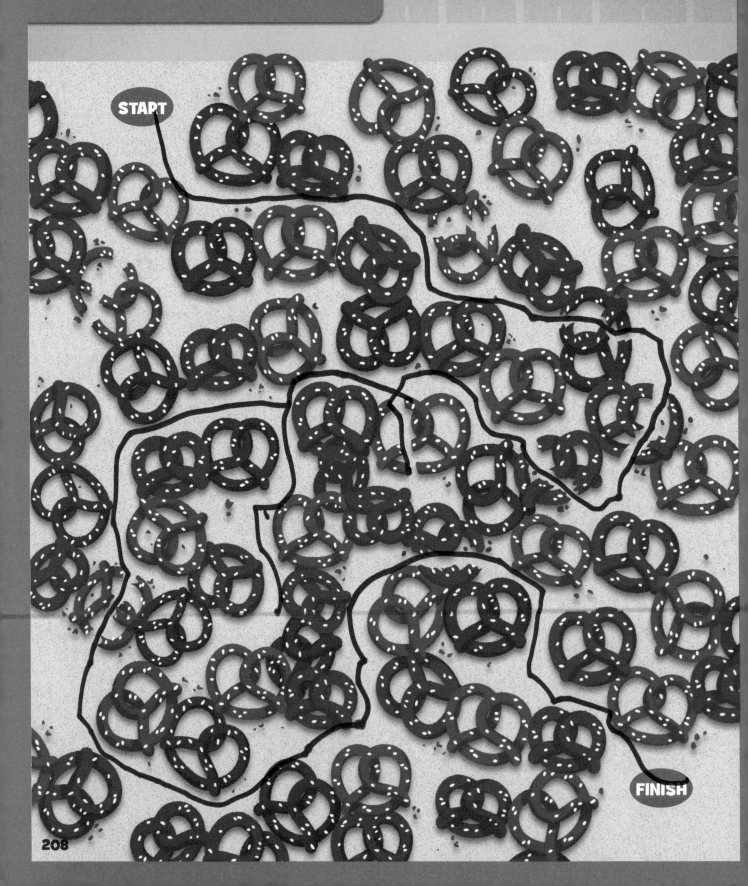

Mr. Robot

Find your way from one hand of the robot to the other hand.

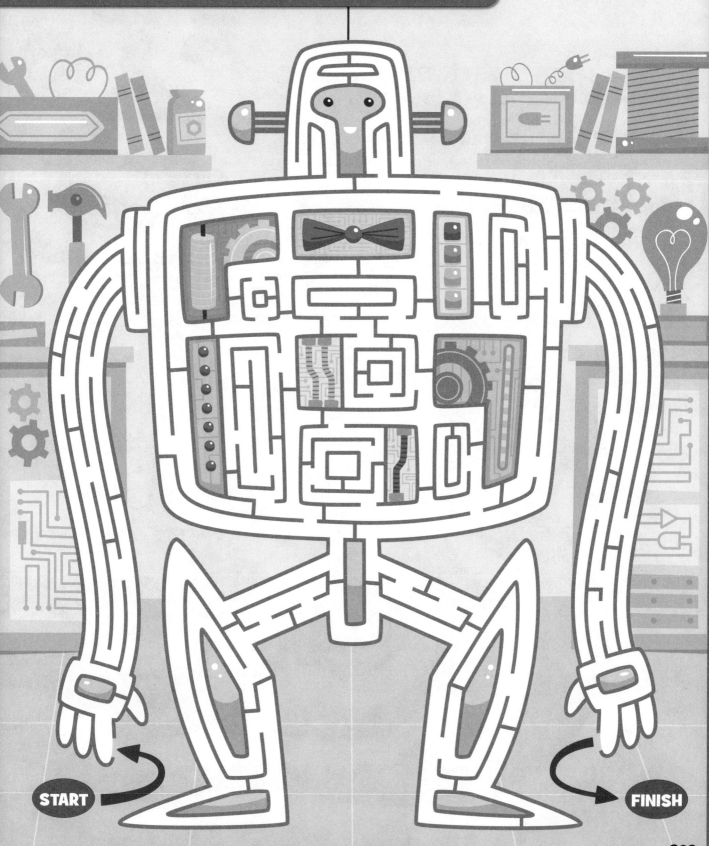

START

FINISH

Paddle Paths

Emma and her dog, Zan, are paddling through the rain forest. Can you help them find the route to their campsite? When you're done, see if you can find at least 10 animals hidden in this scene.

START

FINISH

Birdhouse

Follow the flight path of these birds to see where each bird lives.

Treasure Hunt

Can you find a path to the buried treasure? Start at the 5 in the top corner. You may move to a new box by adding **5** or subtracting **3**. Move up, down, left, or right.

START

5	10	17	10	7	12
5	7	12	13	4	9
11	6	9	8	21	18
16	19	6	11	16	15
13	18	20	12	21	12
10	15	17	15	20	17

FINISH

Black Hills Thrills

Get in gear and help these two bikers make it up the hill and over to town.

START

FINISH

HOTEL

Five Sides

Fitz's favorite number is five. He has just finished drawing a maze with five sides. Help him get out of this perplexing pentagon, and when you're done, see if you can spot five sets of five things in this scene.

START

FINISH

Moose Pals

Help Mort go on the right path to find Murray.
The symbols tell him which way to move.

 Move 1 space down

Move 1 space up

Move 1 space right

Move 1 space left

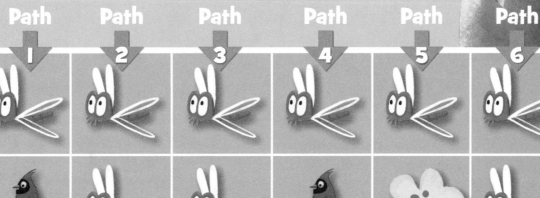

Path 1 **Path 2** **Path 3** **Path 4** **Path 5** **Path 6**

City Stops

Time's ticking! The bus driver has a busy schedule. Follow the maze to each stop on the bus's route, and follow the directions at each site to answer the riddle at the bottom.

4 - POINT FOUNTAIN

STOP 1:
Four people board the bus at the 4-Point Fountain. Put an E in the blank that matches the number of people now on board.

START
The bus driver has four passengers in the back. Put a D in the blank that matches the number of people on board. (Don't forget the bus driver!)

The RIGHT ANGLE RESTAURANT

STOP 3:
Seven hungry people get off at the Right Angle Restaurant, and three people get on. The driver waits for two more people to board. Put a T in the correct blank.

MUSEUM OF MODERN MATH

STOP 2:
Three people get off the bus at the Museum of Modern Math, and two hop on. Put an A in the correct blank.

PYTHAGORAS PUBLIC LIBRARY

STOP 5:
Four book lovers depart at Pythagoras Public Library. Put an O in the correct blank.

STOP 4:
One person gets off at Prime Square, and two people with a lot of shopping bags board. Put an H in the correct blank.

PRIME SQUARE

PERFECT PLUS PARK

FINISH
Last stop. All but one passenger leaves. Put an R in the correct blank. Have you answered the riddle?

What runs through a city without ever moving?

__ __ __ __ __ __ __
6 7 9 2 3 8 5

Art by Mike Dammer

219

Leaping Lizard

This little lizard got on the roof! Help it crawl down the building and find its way back inside to its friends.

START

FINISH

Animal Tracks

Follow each set of tracks to the animal that made them.

Zigzag through the Ziggurat

The Murray family is vacationing in Mexico and visiting the famous pyramids. Help them climb to the top by finding the right path.

START

FINISH

Dog Run

Buster wants to meet up with his friends at the dog park. Can you help him sniff out the trail that will take him there?

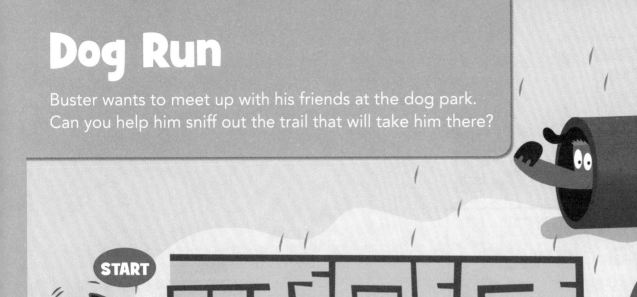

START

FINISH

Go Team!

The Typhoon soccer team is heading to the big championship game. Help their bus get to the stadium. Keep an eye out for the one-way streets!

Super Savers

This community is lucky enough to have four fantastic superheroes to help in times of need. Follow the path to take each superhero where he or she needs to go.

Answers

Page 4

Page 5

Pages 6–7

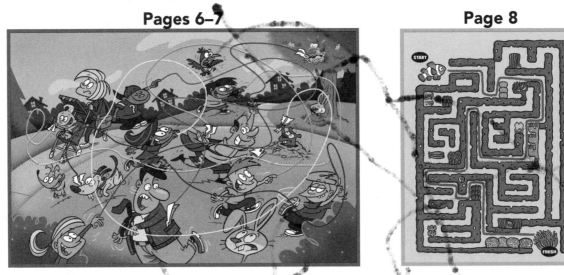

Page 8

Page 9

Pages 10–11

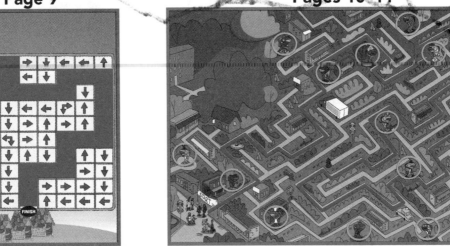

Page 12

Page 13

Here is one path we found. You may have found more.

Pages 14–15

A KNIGHT LIGHT

Page 16

Page 17

Pages 18–19

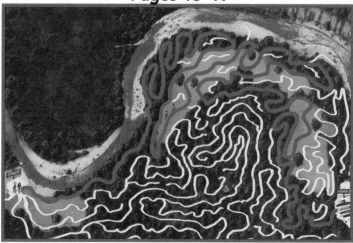

Answers

Page 20

Page 21

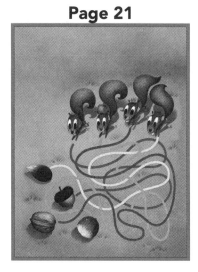

Pages 22–23

Page 24

Page 25

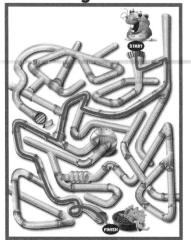

Pages 26–27

Answers

Page 28

Page 29

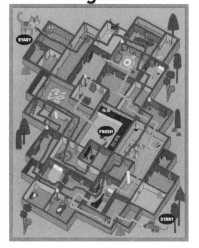

Pages 30–31

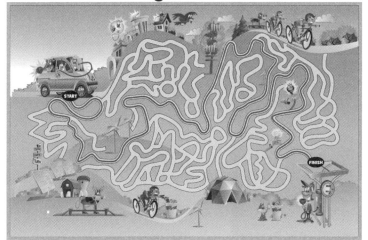

Page 32

Page 33

Pages 34–35

What's a robot's favorite party snack?
MIXED NUTS

Answers

Page 36

Page 37

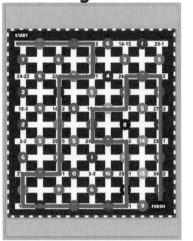

Pages 38–39

Page 40

drill, grill, hill, bill, spill, windmill, chill

Page 41

*train, crane, mane, cane,
Great Dane, weather vane*

Pages 42–43

Answers

Page 44

Page 45

Pages 46–47

Page 48

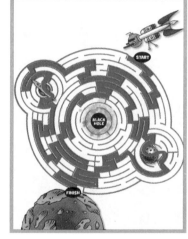

Page 49

Pages 50–51

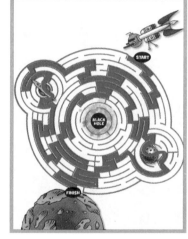

Answers

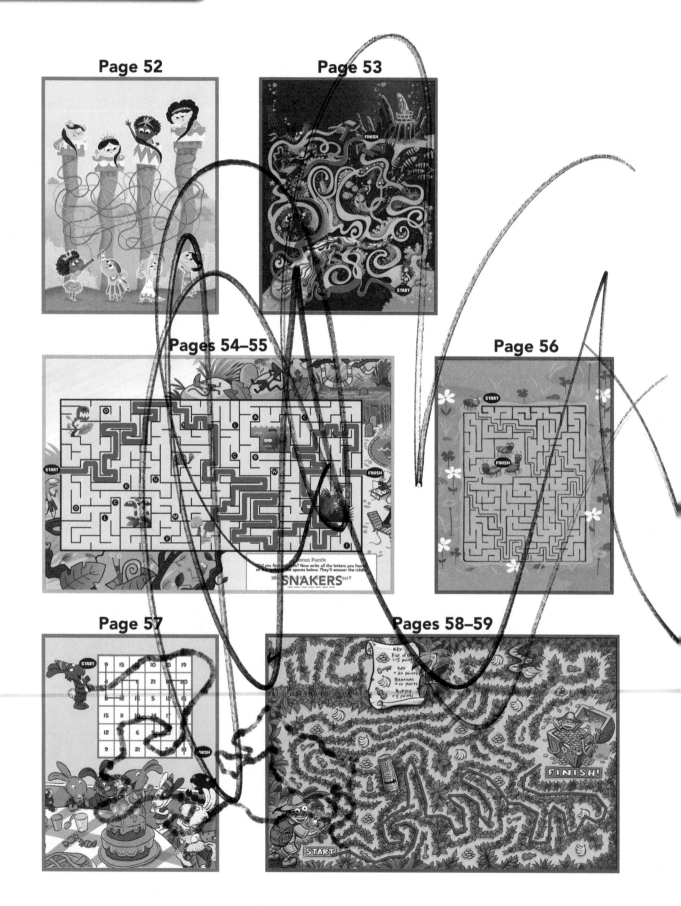

Page 52

Page 53

Pages 54–55

Page 56

Page 57

Pages 58–59

Answers

Page 60

1. Twelve

2. Stool, skateboard, shovel, stroller, stone, sundial

3. Benches by the fountain, pillars, green triangular trees, brown dogs, bird baths

4. More people before the fountain

Page 61

Pages 62–63

KOALA, GORILLA, KANGAROO

Page 64

Page 65

Pages 66–67

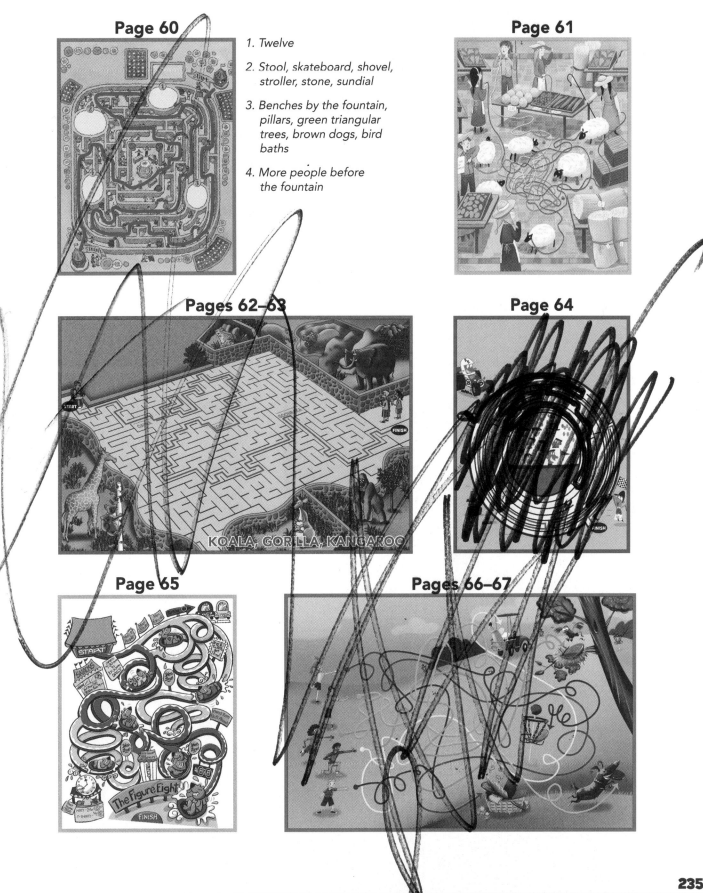

Answers

Page 68

Page 69

Pages 70–71

Page 72

Page 73

Pages 74–75

Bonus Puzzle
Once you've found the correct path, write the letters along it in order in the spaces below. They'll answer this riddle:

What is a scarecrow's favorite fruit?

STRAW=BERRIES

Answers

Page 76

Page 77

Here is one path we found. You may have found more.

Pages 78–79

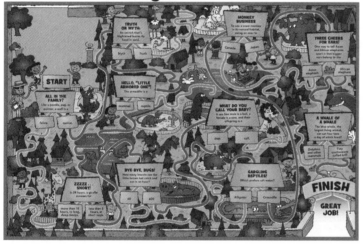

Page 80

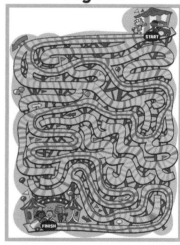

Page 81

Pages 82–83

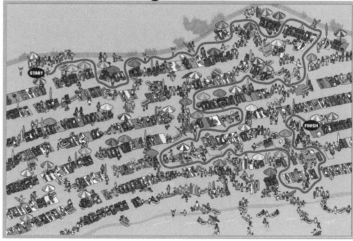

Answers

Page 84

Page 85

Pages 86–87

Page 88

Page 89

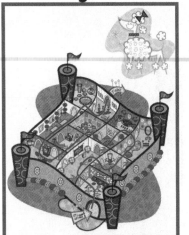

Pages 90–91

Pages 92–93

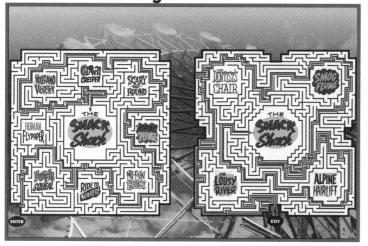

Pages 94–95

Page 96

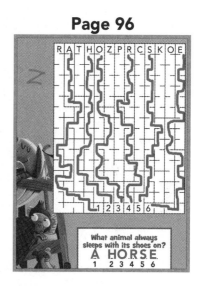

Page 97

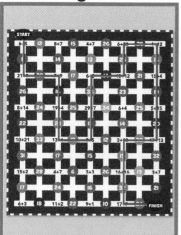

Pages 98–99

Answers

Page 100

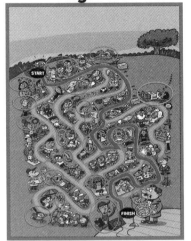

Page 101

Pages 102–103

Page 104

Page 105

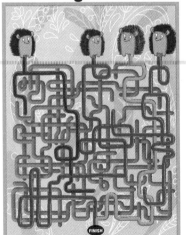

Pages 106–107

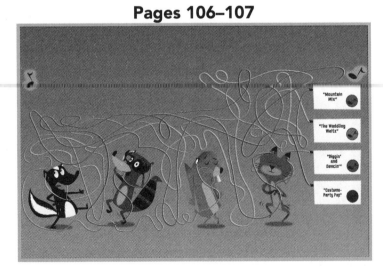

Answers

Page 108

Page 109

Pages 110–111

Page 112

Page 113

Pages 114–115

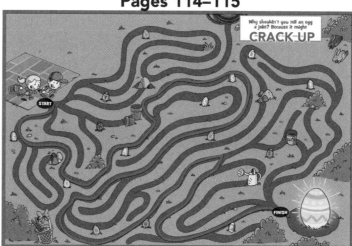

Why shouldn't you tell an egg
a joke? Because it might
CRACK-UP

Answers

Page 116

Page 117

Pages 118–119

Page 120

Page 121

Pages 122-123

Answers

Page 124

Page 125

Pages 126–127

Page 128

Page 129

Pages 130–131

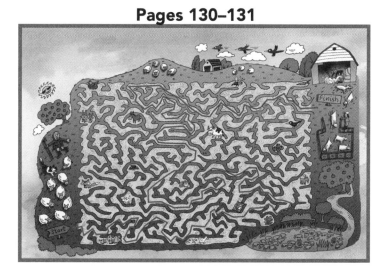

Answers

Page 132

Page 133

Pages 134–135

Page 136

Page 137

Pages 138–139

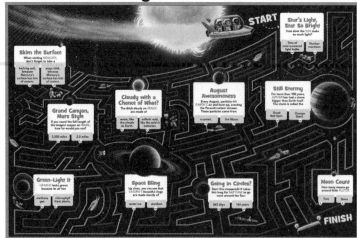

Answers

Page 140

Page 141

Pages 142–143

Page 144

Page 145

Pages 146–147

Answers

Page 148

Page 149

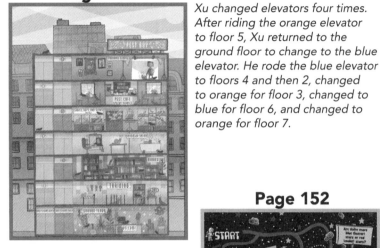

Xu changed elevators four times. After riding the orange elevator to floor 5, Xu returned to the ground floor to change to the blue elevator. He rode the blue elevator to floors 4 and then 2, changed to orange for floor 3, changed to blue for floor 6, and changed to orange for floor 7.

Pages 150–151

Page 152

There are more blue stars.
Riddle 1: Astro-nut
Riddle 2: You rocket
Riddle 3: Because it was full
Riddle 4: Unidentified frying object

Page 153

Pages 154–155

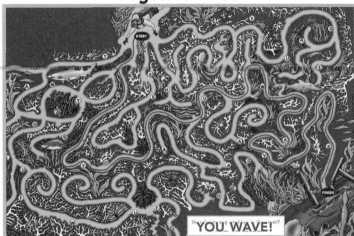

Answers

Page 156

RATZEROBCRKOA

1	2	3	4	5	6

If the alphabet goes from A to Z, what goes from Z to A?

A ZEBRA

Page 157

Pages 158–159

Page 160

Page 161

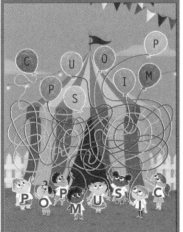

Pages 162–163

247

Answers

Page 164

Page 165

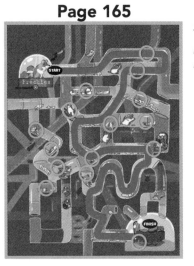

Super Bonus!

mat, star, ham, hat, heat, seat, heart, haste, rat, tear, earth

Pages 166–167

Page 168

Page 169

Pages 170–171

Answers

Page 172

Page 173

Pages 174–175

Page 176

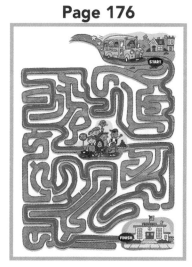

Page 177

Pages 178–179

Answers

Page 180

rake, cider, apple, pumpkin

Page 181

Pages 182–183

Page 184

Page 185

Pages 186–187

Page 188

Page 189

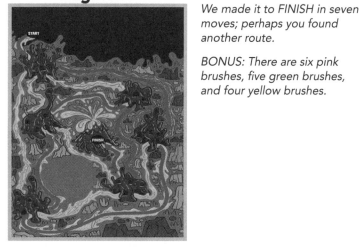

We made it to FINISH in seven moves; perhaps you found another route.

BONUS: There are six pink brushes, five green brushes, and four yellow brushes.

Pages 190–191

Page 192

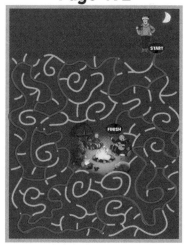

Page 193

Pages 194–195

Answers

Page 196

Page 197

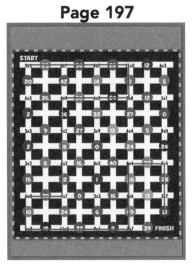

Pages 198–199

Page 200

Page 201

Pages 202–203

Answers

Page 204

What is a basketball player's favorite cheese?
S W I S H
1 2 3 4 5

Page 205

Pages 206–207

Page 208

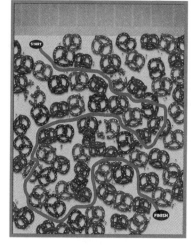

Page 209

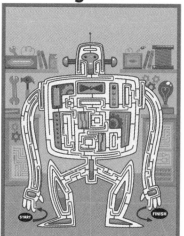

Pages 210–211

Answers

Page 212

Page 213

Pages 214–215

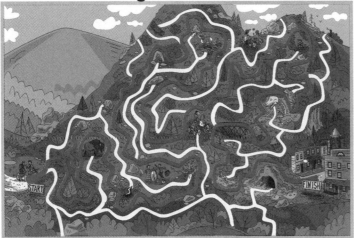

Page 216

Page 217

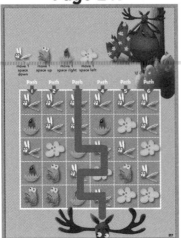

Pages 218–219

Answers

Page 220

Page 221

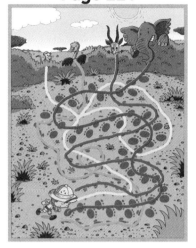

Pages 222–223

Page 224

Page 225

Pages 226–227

For information about permission to reprint selections from this book,
please contact permissions@highlights.com.

Published by Highlights for Children
P.O. Box 18201
Columbus, Ohio 43218-0201
Printed in the United States of America
ISBN: 978-1-62979-884-4

Cover art by Galia Bernstein